In Darkness the Seed of Light

Simon Loughlin

Cover photo by: Angus Massey and Daphna Saker Massey

Cover Design by Maria Kilina

Chapter sketches by: Lourdes Nuñez del Rio

For Aly,

for whom this book was written,

because she wanted to know the story of the windows

Rickshaw Driver

Night has come; now the leaping fountains speak more loudly. And my soul too is a leaping fountain.

Night has come; now all the songs of lovers awaken. And my soul too is the song of a lover.

Something unstilled, unstillable is within me; it wants to be voiced. A craving for love is within me; it speaks the language of love.

—Friedrich Nietzche
Thus Spoke Zarathustra

Paharganj was supposed to be a jump-off point, not a destination. After all, who would choose to stay in the noisiest, dirtiest hub on the planet, a bewildering throng of touts, beggars and hashish vendors, of long-bearded fortune-tellers selling the future and dubious holy men in orange robes selling liberation, streets where dazed tourists are continually swarmed by a frenzy of sales' pitches and emotional blackmail, where emaciated cows range freely chewing organic refuse and plastic bottles, where Chai Wallahs and fast-food vendors squat beside open sewers as they prepare their fare, their heads level with the exhausts of the motor rickshaws rattling through the dusty, potholed alleys with ever-honking horns. Here the world mills together in one unified mass of chaos, trying to score a few rupees, trying to score a hit, trying to find a guru who might make sense of it all, looking for a mouthful of food to ease the gnawing in the guts. Paharganj in the centre of Delhi is a place for travellers to pass through, a place to get an onward ticket, to crash before an early morning train, a place you plan to get out of as soon as possible. But I hadn't planned—was no longer capable of planning, suffering serious sleep deprivation and emotional burnout. In the previous two days, I had separated from my wife and son, knowing it was possibly forever and said goodbye to a beloved dying relative knowing it certainly was.

Over the previous year, my familiar life had descended into domestic hell, and India had promised salvation for two reasons. First, I wanted to find the place of a recurrent vision I was having, a vision of a physical space, a place I was convinced that existed somewhere in India. The place of the vision was deeply peaceful. The air was pure and prayer flags fluttered lightly through some natural stone windows, beyond which were majestic tree-lined mountains, landscapes framed by the windows, ever subtly changing with the light of the sky and shifting clouds. While all around me had been jealousy, anger and despair, I had often taken refuge in that vision, gone there in my imagination, a place where I simply felt peace. The vision had remarkable consistency. When it vanished, I would often wonder where it was and the more I thought of it, the more I became convinced it was in India, possibly somewhere on the lower slopes of the Himalayas. Maybe it was a temple, maybe it was a monastery, maybe simply the home of some benevolent soul—I wasn't sure. What I did feel sure of was that it was the place of my inner healing for all that had gone wrong living with my wife and young son in the mountains.

My second reason for coming to India was to be and travel with my deranged soul-buddy Danny, a man who, through the magic of his laughter, had the ability to make light of absolutely anything. Danny had been travelling in India for the last year and had been calling me frequently to talk about a Russian woman he'd fallen in love with. It was all new to him, this infatuation, this obsession with one woman. They made love all the time he said, and he couldn't get enough and she couldn't get enough. 'It's so . . .' he would tell me on the phone, but so *what* he couldn't articulate. He was phoning me because he was convinced I was the only one who would understand. 'I told the lads, but they just looked at me as if to say . . . and?' On the phone, he would try to describe her essence but inevitably ended up repeating the story of her feet up the wall and them in such ecstatic union that they didn't care her friend was in the room . . .

'She's so . . . she's so . . .' he would stammer, struggling for the words to make sense of it all.

'She's so Russian!'

So many hours and rupees on long-distance calls he'd spent to describe her to me, and all I knew was that she was Russian! She had flown to India three times now to meet him and they had been together day and night for the last two months. I was curious to meet her, to say the least.

We met in a rooftop restaurant in Paharganj. I hardly recognised Danny at first. He seemed stressed—he had lost hair and grown a frown. He let me know straight away that they wouldn't be staying, that they would be off in the morning to Nepal to renew visas. His Russian beloved, on the other hand, looked like the proverbial cat that had got the cream. She was blonde and well proportioned and her movements were silk smooth as though everything gave her pleasure. She seemed reluctant to talk and spent most of the time staring at a game on her mobile phone. During the evening, I asked her three basic questions:

'What is your name?'

'My name is Natasha.'

'Where do you live?'

'I live in Moscow.'

'What do you do there?'

'I am interior designer.'

Danny and I spent the rest of our time in the restaurant catching up. Natya (as Danny called her) soon got bored and went to bed, and Danny and I decided to go out for a chai. On the street, he suddenly became animated and started hopping up and down like an agitated chimp.

'I never knew all this!' he proclaimed.

'Never knew all what?'

'All those things she told you—I didn't know.'

All what things? All I had asked her was her name, where she was from and her profession. In all the months of bliss they had spent together, Danny hadn't got around to it—I began to wonder if I really had understood the full import of what he had been trying to tell me during our long-distance phone calls.

It wasn't long before Danny's agitation got the better of him. 'She will be wondering where I am,' he explained, leaving me alone in the nighttime alley wondering the same. In the morning, as they packed up, we made some hurried plans to meet up soon in Varanasi. Then they were off. It was to be the last time I would see them.

With the excitement of seeing Danny now past, sleep deprivation hit me like a sledgehammer and yet, still I could not sleep. Certain faculties had gone into deep sleep—like the ability to make decisions and the ability to make conversation. I felt like I ought to be getting out of Paharganj, but the organisational powers necessary to arrange an onward ticket seemed beyond me, especially considering that I had no idea where to go. No place pulled me more than another. I realised that I had been assuming Danny would take care of that and that I would have just gone along happily for the ride.

Sleeplessness persisted for a whole week. Due to the time change, my habitual sleep time came around dawn in the new time zone, a dawn whose vague smog-filtered light was accompanied by honkings, clangings, yelling and the roaring of exhaust-damaged vehicles, a din that intensified with the light to soon render all hope of sleep impossible.

All I could do was watch it all. I watched it as though it were a dream, a dream I did not take part in. By night, I watched from the window of my room in a cheap hotel which overlooked a chaotic roundabout, in the centre of which sat some strange power hub, with ten-metre high rusty pylons and a mass of humming boxes in no obvious order, all grimed black with neglect. A thousand cables ran out from the centre, creating a chaotic electrically charged spider's web, ready to fry any unwary monkey or man. Ramshackle billboards crowded the crumbling façades around—opposite, the 'Lovely Store', below, the 'Dollar Club'.

All night long, I watched as wild dogs formed packs and took control around midnight, as the human throng dwindled to nothing. The same skinny, mangy beasts that, during daylight, cowered individually beneath mobile food stalls and in any available dirt space at the street-side now howled and gashed ferociously without cease, the new kings of sheltering darkness. No longer the gauntlet of touts and vendors ever threatening to draw on rupees, now gnashing and drooling, the dogs took up the files, ever threatening to draw on the blood of any soul with the daring or misfortune to walk it. I watched as such nervous tiptoeing figures traced the wide-arcing paths of maximum distance from the lines of bared teeth. I vaguely considered the possibility of having to help, should the files collapse upon a victim, for I imagined I was the only observer of the drama.

I watched too the coming and going of large, rusty trucks, whose motors ran outside the window at 3 a.m. For no good reason other than sleep-starved paranoia, I kept imagining that one might contain a car bomb for this hotel, populated as it was by Westerners, including many Americans and Israelis. My reasoning function, which thought in terms of probabilities, was not awake enough to come to my aid. I experienced a strangely naked fear, a fear which was projecting based on images from popular media, a media which thrives on paranoia.

During the daytime, I had no idea what to do. There had just been a desperation to escape the demons. There had been something to run from, but, other than a vision of a place that might be anywhere on the planet, I had nothing to run to. Sometimes, I wandered into the streets and alleys, lifted by an urge to move, that and a hope that I might find some sign that would point the way to where I was supposed to go, a place my only impression of which being that it was somewhere else. What I found on these sleepwalks was an eclectic collection of Indian souls and briefly, a splendid new career.

The first of these souls was an old man wearing a western

collared shirt and carrying a large code-locked leather briefcase, his eyes appearing to look far beyond the chaos around him; I couldn't help but notice him. When we made eye contact, he approached me and said we should go for a chai. In the comparative calm of a kerosene-smoke blackened tea shop, I made Babu's acquaintance. He proceeded to open the leather briefcase, to open to me the woes of his existence. The suitcase contained a sheaf of papers detailing his ongoing court cases that would, according to him, return his deserved position in life, that of wealth and grace. The Dacoits had robbed him and beat him he told me, in his unusual accent, with hints of English upper-class, they had beat him and then dumped him unconscious 50 km outside the city. The police had failed to protect him—all the details down now on stamped paper, he had a date in court for February, and therefore, he had hope. The woman he rented his piano to had not returned it, and he had a stamped paper for that too. He had lost his money and been evicted from his luxury flat—now he must stay in a hotel where the floors are dirty and wash from a filled bucket! An undeserved fall from grace for a talented musician, a musician who had played sitar and tabla in the embassies of Europe, alongside the great Ravi Shankar no less. Babu talked and I listened, from time to time wondering what my part in all of it was. If he wanted something from me, he didn't make it clear—maybe just a sympathetic ear. He did, however, have one special piece of advice for me.

'Never trust a rickshaw driver. All rickshaw drivers here are bad men.'

One minute out of the chai shop where we had shared a spicy milk tea, and my concerns for Babu's woes had evaporated. Every pair of eyes it seemed sought mine in a plea for today's dinner, for the bus ticket back to the Tibetan homeland, for the operation that mother urgently needs. Amid the throng, my eyes were caught by the sight of a baby crawling through the dirt at the roadside, a baby quickly grabbed by a ragged beggar woman who proceeded to ask me for rupees. Instinctively, I dived into a café—dived into a private space with a fan and waiters cum bodyguards to shelter me from the mass of need outside. I sat down at a table and ordered food. When I looked up, I saw the beggar woman still standing outside the café, looking in at me. As I met her engaging eyes, I felt a certainty that essentially there wasn't much difference between us, nothing that a wash and a few rupees couldn't remedy. I waved to her to come in sit at my table, motioning to my mouth with the first three fingertips of my right hand, the Indian gesture for eating. The waiter looked over at me, suddenly very concerned—an untouchable in his café! Seeking a solution, he asked, 'You want to give her food?' . . . Indian quick mind . . . 'I bring her **Dal** Rice, sir—OK? OK na?' Soon, she had a small plastic bag of lentils and rice, which she ate standing on the street, sharing with the baby and another beggar. From time to time she smiled over at me as she ate. We had dinner together, ten metres apart.

During one somnambulation, I became friendly with a cycle rickshaw driver—despite Babu's warnings I was struck by the feeling that there was something noble in this young man who taxied the rich, the lazy and the less able-bodied, pedalled them on a plush high chair mounted atop his three-wheeled, wrought-iron behemoth, pedalled them kilometres through the rough-surfaced chaotic streets under his own leg-power, all for the price of a handful of bread. He had asked me did I want a tour of the city while I had been aimlessly wandering the streets, my mind 10,000 miles away in problematic relationships, in unsolvable futures. I hadn't wanted a tour of the city, but there was something strong and vital in his eyes, something that finally brought me to where I was. I accepted. The driver introduced himself as Maku. He wanted to take me to a local temple and as I had no alternative in mind, I let him do so; as I sat in a comfortable chair, the sinewy young man pedalled proudly through four lanes of chaotic traffic, swerving to avoid potholes and ducking in and out of tight sewer-lined alleys for shortcuts.

The temple he took me to was a building covered in domes and spires of varying dimensions. It was painted white and it was clean, sitting at odds with the hectic filth-lined highway outside. Inside were varying chambers, each with a statue of Hindu gods and goddesses. My first impression was that it would be a fine place for children to visit. I wondered from chamber to chamber more or less disinterestedly until, standing in front of the statue of one Goddess I suddenly felt rooted to the spot. Her eyes seemed terribly real, overpoweringly beautiful—I felt hypnotised by them and stood staring into them for some minutes. I couldn't resist a surprise stirring in my heart, a great attraction—

for a clay-figure! The intensity of these feelings took me by surprise; I could only liken it to feelings of being in love and at the same time being loved, a feeling of the presence of the feminine in her unadulterated purity, of being in the presence of compassion—a feeling accompanied by my own sensation of lightness. Logically it made no sense, and the strength of the feelings I was having briefly set off alarm bells in what ration was left in my mind. Now, I felt like I had a choice—the choice between running into the cold known of logic or simply accepting this warm loving feeling regardless of where it came from. Maybe because I was looking for transformation by whatever means of a life that seemed to be in tatters, or maybe because my sleep-starved brain was too tired to apply the necessary logic; either way, I just allowed the feelings to be.

It was a familiar sensation and, in feeling it, I remembered it was what I lived for, remembered that I had once felt like this for my wife. Once she too had been an infallible Goddess to me, yet in recent times, whenever such feelings had arisen in her presence, I had suppressed them, for fear of their power and the unpredictable objects of their focus—a focus that was not always her.

Leaving the temple, I felt re-energised. For the journey back, I asked Maku if I could pedal. Maku happily agreed and climbed into the backseat with a big smile and a warning to pull over at the junctions, to allow him to handle them. At first, the rickshaw felt awkward—it only had one gear. With the weight of carriage and passenger, it took a great force to turn the pedals. This force would cause the rickshaw to lurch its weight from one rear wheel and then to the other; it moved in a continual side to side swaying. My first reaction was to stop this motion, use my strength to straighten it up, but I soon realised that all the traffic around us was swaying too, then what had seemed chaos took on a light swaying order. The traffic wasn't the linear motion I was used to, but a less hurried, more rhythmic motion. I swayed towards narrow gaps as they opened, and they would open wider; there was protest from no one as I did so. Maku seemed pleased with my progress and did not object as I entered the junctions— four lanes of dense, chaotic traffic merging into four lanes of chaotic traffic at a right angle without a road sign in sight!

The journey ended under a large dusty banyan tree on the outskirts of Paharganj, a place which Maku called home. I felt exhilarated, for the first time in days, feeling wide awake, more awake than I had felt for months. I arranged to hire the rickshaw for the whole of the next day—now the thought of a city tour held great appeal—and I would pedal it myself! I left Maku with enough rupees to buy a coat, which sleeping outside in winter he badly needed, an amount equivalent to the price of one beer back in Europe.

The next morning, I collected the rickshaw as arranged and set out for my grand city tour with no particular destinations in mind. I didn't get far before an old man with a pair of very thick glasses flagged me down—wanted a ride to the metro station. Had his limited eyesight taken me to be a local driver? I was struck dumb and watched in silent awe as he delicately mounted the carriage. He spoke something in Hindi, the only words I understood being 'metro station', to which I nodded in agreement and tentatively pushed the pedals, lurching the rickshaw into motion. The old man looked fragile and vulnerable sitting unsecured in the high chair at the back—with the air of one looking to more ethereal realities. I felt nervous, for sure he wouldn't survive a tumble to the ground. I drove with care, shouting 'metro station' to amused pedestrians, who guided me with smiles and pointing arms at every junction. With a sense of purpose, I wound my way through the thick throng of pedestrians, swerved to the sides to avoid the heavier and faster motor rickshaws, who bore horn- honking straight towards us without swerving. As diplomatically as possible, I shoved open a passage between two matronly buffaloes standing side by side. All the while, I took care to keep the rear wheels out of the sewers and the biggest of the potholes. By the time we reached the metro station, all the sleeplessness had been completely washed from my body—my whole being tingled, I felt exhilarated and vibrant. The old man gave me enough money for a handful of bread and handed me a lighted beedi—a local cigarette of tobacco rolled in a dried leaf. I don't usually smoke, but that cigarette I accepted. We smoked together in silence and then he left with a simple nod.

By late afternoon, I had taxied many passengers and knew some routes between the more common destinations. As an obvious foreigner, I had no problem finding custom. The passengers delighted in crowding the backseat to bursting, in telling me to go faster, in prodding me with their feet, in overpaying me, in underpaying me, in inviting me for a chai . . . they delighted and I delighted. Even touts would occasionally get on, using their hired minutes as windows through which to advertise their wares.

I felt a little uneasy about taking custom from the local rickshaw drivers. It was with great trepidation that I first approached a rank of waiting rickshaws, peevishly making my way to the back of the queue, but to my surprise, they welcomed me with open arms. After being re-fuelled with some cups of sweet tea from the flask of another driver, I was issued to the front of the queue, amidst a flurry of smiles and handshakes from the other drivers. When the next passengers approached, some other drivers took care of fare negotiation on my behalf and then gave me instructions on how to reach my destination.

I continued to work like this for a few days, feeling energised and alive. Often, my rides felt like a carnival procession. In busy streets, many of the cars would honk their horns and shout greetings and encouragement. Some were full of praise and encouragement while others questioned my mental health.

Rickshaw life continued into the evening also—sometimes I would go with Maku on his errands; we would alternate as passenger and driver. His new vantage point from the raised chair delighted him as much as pedalling him through the crazy streets thrilled me. 'Everyone is shouting "Kaun Ho?"' he laughed from the high chair one day as I pedalled him through a densely packed neighbourhood 'Kaun Ho?—"Who is this?"'

After such evening forays, I returned to my room and, eventually, to my zombie-like state. Despite the exhilaration of the day, by night, in my dingy hotel room behind a closed door, the phantoms of my recent past returned to ensure continued sleeplessness. Concerns about my wife and son and a sense of futility merged in a foggy mental blur—a blur that I had no energy to transcend. I took up my usual vigil on the nighttime roundabout, occasionally my consciousness drifting to other places, never sure if I was dreaming— dreaming of the roundabout or any other place. I longed for my mind to stop! I longed for sleep, deep, dreamless sleep. Night after night, sleep eluded me and yet, each time the grating mechanical racket of dawn came, and with it, the promise of new alleys, new passengers and the enlivening burning in my thighs, I would feel as though I had woken up, the excitement of another day of rickshaw taxiing lifting me fresh from the bed.

As I was beginning to wonder if this was the reason I had come to India, so fulfilled with my work I felt, it came to an end. My celebrity it seemed ran before me—too soon my fame reached the police—who began to demand payment of fines for dubious crimes such as 'riding in unauthorised zones', for 'transporting without license', for 'working without a permit'. The accusation always varied, but the solution remained the same— payment! The fines always exceeded my day's takings. Then one day, while I was out taxiing, they fined Maku for renting his vehicle to a foreigner without a license. That evening, I found him very stressed; he said they had taken all his money and would come back for more the following day if I continued to 'work'. For me it all had little consequence, but now, it was threatening the livelihood of Maku and so ended a brief but fulfilling career.

Walking back from returning the rickshaw for the last time, I spontaneously bought a bus ticket from a travel agent; a task that some days previous had been an endless process of frustrated decision making, now, feeling inspired and invigorated from days of rickshaw adventures, that task was carried out in an instant. My mind temporarily free of the baggage of history, the next step was simple, obvious, arrived without my need to analyse. Rishikesh, a town in the Himalayan foothills was not so far away—a few hours by bus—and sure to be much quieter than Paharganj, a place where I would surely sleep!

His Story
I

He dreamt of peace, he dreamt of the place which embraced it, the place where it might find nourishment and grow. That place was dream, and by day he dreamt that dream might never end. Where Peace was, there would be his Home.

He had been a warrior for too long—his war was the war against Fear itself. The long drawn out battles were beginning to exhaust his body and spirit. His rebellion took the form of running—he would travel the surface of the earth for months on end under his own energies, suffering cold and rains, suffering long spells of loneliness and hunger—and so he lived. He was running from the Voice of Fear—which seemed to pervade his mind and the mind of others, the Voice of Fear, which speaks thus:

'It is a free world and you are free to define your limitations. But define them you must! And define them within our limitations. Sign the contract and hold in front of your nose so that you know who you are, so we may know who you are. We will punch a pinhole in it so the light may reach you, a single ray along which you may see your whole future. You cannot love these, you cannot love those . . . if you love an object, then you are condemned to obedience to that object as long as your body persists—no matter how that object behaves. You must learn *allegiance—by which we mean, closing your eyes and ears to everything else. You must place yourself en contra all that threatens to transform the objects of your stated allegiance. Finally there is death, and there you may find your heaven, but for now—blinkers! For now, a pinhole on heaven to sustain you! For now, hand over responsibility to authority—the authority of time and establishment, which knows better.'*

The 'Voice of Fear' ever coaxed him towards fixed addresses and professions, towards enumerated persona and archetypes of legal amorous contact, of valid prejudice. The Voice suggested he should be neatly categorised and filed by the machines, while dangling the carrot of 'Security' before him, security which the Voice itself created a need for by its seeming omnipresence and subtly threatening manner. The Voice negated his infinite potential, beckoned him to replace it with blind reliance. The Voice took a large space in his mind.

Driving back the Voice's invasion was his life's battle. How many times had Fear spoken to him and his beloved, entered them like a slow creeping cancer, forced him to run to the purities of solitude and wilderness. The battles dragged on for years; he had to abandon the woman that had once been his healing, his life force, his source of bliss. Until he was truly free of fear, he could not truly love.

The Voice drove him to pedal a bicycle alone through the deserts and mountains of foreign lands. There, after long drawn out physical struggles, the mind would finally go quiet—and suddenly he would become aware of the great spaces around him. Suddenly, they would feel alive—deeply present. These moments were victories over negativity, over Fear—these were moments of realisation of his true nature. These moments were what sustained him.

The battles were hard-fought. They dragged on for years, years turning into decades. He knew that his fighting spirit was finite, that finally, within himself, he had to find a place where he might heal, he had to find Peace. That place of Peace, if it were to exist on the earth—that place was his home.

Asylum

"My Dear Sancho, there is nothing in this world so strange as to be unbelievable"

-Miguel de Cervantes, Don Quixote

I arrived in Rishikesh at nighttime and took a room in a guest house on the jungle-clad hill behind the town. Quiet it was indeed—no more packs of barking dogs, no exhaust-free running motors and honking horns; the only noise was the wind as it blew down from the Himalayas, but still I could not sleep!

The silence filled with the echoes of my wife's anger, her accusations. They seemed so petty—but they had been relentless—and finally, I had succumbed to the same. She had once meant everything to me—I had tried to throw off my past life that I might have more life with her, dropped contact with friends and family, and left a successful business because her eyes had hinted at something much greater. It had come to month-long screaming arguments about hair in the bath or a casual message written to another woman. The magic that I had felt with her here in India—where had it gone? I had to make sense of it before I could find my peace. I lay awake and listened to the wind in the branches; I went for a walk in the moonlight and watched its reflection in the waters of the Ganges, the river they considered a Goddess, the river they called 'Mother'. There wasn't a soul to be seen anywhere.

In the absence of proper sleep, I never felt truly awake. I began to exist in a trance-like state. For days I sat motionless for long periods—at roadside tea stalls and on benches, but most of all in a hotel courtyard near my room, the place where I felt most certain I would not be bothered. To my sleep-starved mind, the thought process itself required more energy than I could muster and my mind became more a sequence of mild hallucinations, interrupted only by the occasional bodily necessities. For many days, other than to order food, I spoke to no one. Other people didn't seem real. It reminded me of a sensation I had had as a young child, a strong feeling that there was only my own existence. I watched people vaguely as though I were watching a television program—a program where everything happened as expected, which gave a certain sense of comfort.

I had nothing to do, nowhere to go . . . the world felt like a balloon. Essentially just air, space . . . a thin film at the edge giving an impression of form, sometimes it expanded, sometimes it contracted—but the content remained essentially empty. I too felt like a balloon. I had a vague idea of my appearance, of how others might perceive me. Inside, thoughts and feelings came and went, took form in the aimless space within me and vanished as quickly as they had appeared, sometimes to be replaced by others, sometimes not. Sometimes, the vacuum was filled with the sounds around me. There were the many voices of the other hotel guests talking at once, there was the distant rushing of the river, there was music drifting from one doorway or another . . . they all merged as one. Maybe it was because I was too tired— but I did not focus on any, could not. I stopped trying. A peace began to descend upon me—a peace like the peace I had felt before, sitting in an old ruin in a Spanish mountain forest listening to the wind.

~~~

It was Knud that burst my balloon. He came and sat at my table—a wild intensity in his eyes—and simply asked if he could talk to me. And talk he did—talk and talk and talk—mostly about the menu!

. . . I really had to try the garlic potatoes, and the carrot and coriander soup that was really something special, but I should avoid the risotto . . .

Knud asked me a few questions to which I answered as briefly as possible—I preferred to listen. Knud continued to talk about the menu with an intensity that amused me.

Over the next days, Knud often sat with me; as undiscussed items on the menu dwindled, he began to talk more of his life. He had owned a spiritual book-store in Sweden—he obviously had a passion for spiritual books—every time he sat down, he had a different one with him. He sometimes described them, and when he did so, it was with the same intensity he had described the garlic potatoes.

He had been content in his spiritual bookstore he told me. He had a curtain—behind which he could lie down and read books; if he really got into one, he would just lock the door. Then one day a woman had entered his bookstore and told him that she had dreamt of the place the previous night, and in the dream, Knud had given her the shop. On hearing this tale, Knud immediately gave her the bookshop and never went back!

After that he had some job which didn't suit him so well. 'The people in Sweden are so narrow-minded you know . . .' He didn't bother to explain what the job involved—just that he had needed some time off—stress-related problem, somehow related also to a car accident—he had gone to a psychiatrist for a line. The psychiatrist had apparently classified him as schizophrenic.

'He recommended, "This man is insane and he should not be allowed to work another day in his life."' Knud laughed.

Now, at thirty-something, Knud was pensioned off on a mental disability allowance enabling him to travel the world and read his spiritual books in winter sunshine.

He fed little details of his life like this, not sequenced in time, rather just as they came to him. Whatever Knud talked about, it had the common property of intensity. This intensity combined with his openness was energising. He seemed to express everything in him without hesitation or reservation, revealing all his darkness and light at once. His intensity came from nothing more than a deep will to share it all. This had its effect on me and soon I too began opening to Knud. I told him about what had happened with my wife. Knud criticised nothing—just listened. It had been so long since I had been able to express openly with anyone. As I talked, I felt lighter—a long-suppressed vulnerability began to overtake me. As I talked I would begin to tremble lightly, a trembling that increased the more I expressed. Gradually my defences dropped, until I heard myself telling Knud, 'It's over with her.'

In the instant I said it, I realised that it was the first time I had—and as I said it, without thinking, I put my right hand in the air. Instantly, a beautiful brown red and yellow leaf landed in my palm, a leaf that must have been floating on the wind. Such a beautiful leaf, it stunned me to silence. I felt strong emotion—an intoxicating mixture of beauty and sadness. A leaf that had just let go!

'You see!' Knud laughed a deep rumbling laugh that came from his belly, 'You see!'

I guess the incident proved something from one of his books.

Knud knew everyone in the hotel—and introduced me to them one by one. First there was Stefan—a skinny middle-aged Hungarian who had paid up-front for his room for six months—and paid up-front for a block of hashish the size of a birthday cake. Sometimes, he would cross the road to smoke with his **Baba**. Otherwise, he had no plans to go anywhere, which lent him a certain charm. When the other travellers' conversations turned to the wrangles of future plans, Stefan simply disappeared. He had a habit of magically re-appearing during laughter, music and presence . . . ever a smile on his face. Mostly he was calm and passive, but occasionally, he would get very excited about some unexpected topic.

'Who wins a gunfight', he asked me one day, brimming with an eagerness that I had until then never witnessed, 'the man who draws first or the man who draws second?'

I couldn't reply quickly, so Stefan answered himself, with intoxicating delight, 'The man who draws second—you know why?'

No, I didn't.

'Because he doesn't have to think!'

The oldest guest in the hotel was a vivacious seventy-year-old American Tarot reader and author going by the name of Mama Amore. She had first come to my attention via fliers she had posted everywhere, advertising individual card readings. Her obvious maturity seemed to lend the promised sessions certain credibility. Although I had no particular draw to Tarot, decided to seek her out, partly out of curiosity and partly from a will to try anything to help me come to terms with my relationship demons. I finally found my would-be saviour one morning sitting in the courtyard. She was alone and, despite the early hour, obviously drunk.

'That's love!' she thundered as I approached, pointing at two mangy street dogs humping in front of her table. 'You kids come here to learn about love—that's real love!'

Hoping not to be noticed, I sat down at an adjacent table and ordered a chai, as though that had been the reason for my arrival.

For some reason unknown to me, Mama Amore was Knud's arch enemy. I would know she had entered our space by the sudden twisting of Knud's features into hate-filled disgust. I would turn to find her pulling faces at him like a small child. Unable to continue our conversations at these times Knud could only make strange hissing noises and would often get up and leave without explanation—the only occurrences in my eyes which gave a little credence to his psychiatrist's diagnoses.

Knud also introduced me to Daphna—an artist who photographed what I can only describe as the light behind appearances. One afternoon, as we drank glasses of tea together at a small glass table, I noticed her attention drawn to the sunlight that had passed through the tea and was now playing as white lines over the table. She took out her camera, silently observed for a while, and then clicked. Later that evening she showed me what looked like a white angel floating in space, an angel who had been dancing beside me as I drank tea in the afternoon sunlight, had I only the vision to see Her. Then she showed me photographs of herself taken by her partner, masses of blue light warping and bending light, somehow recognisable as human and in a vague way, recognisable as her, but not her so much as a physical being, but rather as mutable spirit. She explained the process to me in a language that was then new to me, but as I listened, I felt an inner recognition. To look fixedly at a thing for an extended period, the concept the mind holds of it finally dissolves. A reality beyond concepts then emerges, and we begin to see what lies beyond our conceptual mind—a mind that can only see what it has seen before, a mind that is trapped therefore in its own history, a mind therefore that cannot see what actually is. Through seeing this reality, Daphna somehow magically coaxed her camera into capturing it. Even without the camera, Daphna's attention was forever guided to these apparitions; maybe she didn't even have to look for them, they just surrounded her, I couldn't be sure. In her presence, she would occasionally point out lights in unexpected places, and in doing so, open little chinks in my own reality, transport me briefly to an existence beyond name or form. In her presence, I felt a certain awe—a desire to tread softly.

Of all the beautiful souls I encountered in Rishikesh, the one who worked the deepest effect on me was a woman I had barely spoken to—one whose name was Maya!—a silent shining soul that I first saw in a yoga class, a being who radiated beauty, a beauty that came from within. Our eyes had first met in silence, an experience which dislodged me entirely from the complications of my mind, sent me reeling into a sense of expansion. It was the same feeling I had felt on looking into the eyes of the Goddess statue in the temple in Delhi, the same instant, overwhelming sensation of unconditional love. Only on returning to my senses did I consider how uncanny was her physical likeness to that Goddess . . . the dark radiant eyes, the long dark hair, the beatific smile . . . a resemblance which reminded me also of my wife when I had met her and the feeling I had had in her presence.

In Maya´s presence I felt myself to be in a trance—and although often being in that presence, I felt too self-conscious (or maybe just too conscious) to speak. Instinctually, I felt that cumbersome words could only diminish the magic that was around her, the stimulation of my whole being that I experienced by simply being near her. The only time we spoke was to introduce ourselves—she had told me her name, adding that in her language it meant butterfly.

The image of Maya haunted my mind day after day; each time I found myself alone or in a quiet space, her image would be there. But who was it that was haunting me—a woman that walked the streets of Rishikesh, the reminder of how I had once felt for my wife or the clay Goddess taken human form? Could it be coincidence that her name was Maya—a name that to Indians means illusion! Maya, the illusion of outward appearance, the outer temptations that distract us from our inner peace, temptations that have us lifelong chasing that which is finally no more than a projection of our inner life, of itself hollow, illusory. I couldn't help the feeling that in the figure of this woman, the Great Soul had sent me a riddle, a riddle that was to re-emerge time and time again over the coming months.

Martin was another resident that soon captured my attention and affection. A bald-headed Englishman, for me, he had a familiar façade, the façade of no-nonsense sensibility, a well-titled cancer research scientist no less. Yet probe a little deeper and there was talk of beings from the other realm, a realm more real than what we see; there was a certain obsession with Breatharian-ism, the belief that material sustenance was not necessary for us to live, that light alone was enough. He was in short, perhaps the most esoteric of all the folk in residence. He talked a lot about the power of envisioning, envisioning who he wanted to be, where he wanted to travel, who he wanted to meet. To him, this envisioning—astral travel in his words—was more 'real' than the reality of his senses - begging the question of whether he had needed to fly halfway around the world, polluting up the atmosphere to visit Rishikesh.

Martin was also keen for some adventures beyond the confines of his skull, adventures that I could also partake of. We decided to rent two old Indian bikes and ride to the nearby holy town of Haridwar. In leaving Rishikesh for a day, I hoped to temporarily escape a mounting emotional intensity I was experiencing, an intensity that was growing with the opening of my heart, a process that seemed inexorable. In the end, our outing only served to intensify my emotional state, bound as it was with the presence of death.

We had only pedalled our way to the outskirts of Rishikesh when a large funeral cortège impeded our progress. Slowly, we wove our way through hundreds of orange-robed, chanting disciples making their way through the streets, their dead guru floating above them in a shoulder-borne chariot. Lying in a deep bed of flowers and garlands, his face had been painted white and then coloured black around the mouth and eyes, giving him the aspect of a macabre clown.

The next cortège we encountered was military—Indian tanks and troop carriers rumbling heavily along the road; khaki-clad soldiers bearing machine guns and rifles glumly looking on the spiritually intoxicated masses. On seeing them, I thought of Daphna. She had been part of such a machine due to mandatory conscription in her country. It seemed so senselessly at odds with the beautiful and sensitive being I knew that I was suddenly overcome. Tears began to flow as the tanks rumbled by; tears that hadn't flowed for years flowed as I pedalled my way past the files of killing machines that stretched on for over a kilometre. As the tears fell, I pedalled with my head down, feeling an indeterminate sense of shame, keeping my head down to avoid the eyes of the passing souls wrapped in military uniform.

Our third reminder of death was the corpse of a rickshaw driver lying at the side of the road near the outskirts of Haridwar. As I cycled by, I realised that no one was paying it any attention—the scene disturbed me somewhat and after cycling by for some hundred metres, I decided to turn and go back to him, letting Martin know as I did so. On nearing the body, I found it covered in a layer of dust, as though it had been there unmoved for some time. He didn't appear to be breathing and there was some caked blood on his forehead. A length of cloth tied his ankle to the wheel of the rickshaw. At a loss for anything better to do, I decided to clean his face with my drinking water. At the touch of water, his eyes suddenly opened and we stared straight at each other, one as shocked as the other. Then, seeing my water bottle, he grabbed it and drank down its content with the urgency of a drowning man gasping for air. Somewhat shakily, he sat up and looked around confusedly.

By this time, a small crowd had gathered around us in a circle. They wanted to know what Martin and my 'good names' might be and where we were from. None of them paid any attention to the newly risen dead, as though he were not there at all. One wanted me to look at his motorbike as though I ought to be more interested in that. Another serious-looking man informed us in good English that we must leave the scene immediately.

'Why?' I asked him.

'Because the police will come soon and they will make you responsible for this accident,' he spoke as though some wrangles with the police on our part were of greater concern than that of the rickshaw driver at our side whose life may have been in the balance. A few others around him nodded in agreement and encouraged us to leave immediately. Is that the reason everyone is ignoring him, I wondered. Somewhat confused and angry, we gave the rickshaw driver some rupees and another bottle of water and left.

'250 cc!' the motorcyclist proudly informed us as we walked back to our bikes. I had to stifle an urge to smack him in the teeth.

~~~

As sunset approached, we were in Haridwar, sitting on the banks of the Ganges drinking chai. Somehow, I had got to the topic of Dostoyevsky's *Idiot*—a book about a certain prince Mishkin, a character who continually speaks the truth as it comes to him, regardless of the consequences. The people around him are divided in opinion as to whether he is an idiot or a sage, some seeing him as both. When I finished talking about the *Idiot*, I noticed a change in the air; the sun was now setting and people were quietly making their evening *pujas*—offerings to the holy river. For a while, we sat and watched in silence. Drums, cymbals and chimes were sounding from the ashrams on the other side of the river, while simultaneously the birds' evening concert had risen to a crescendo. The unbroken ripples on the water now reflected shards of sunset amber in the rivulets that ran between the streaks of white water. The day had ended and the night not yet begun—we had entered the timeless crack that lies between the two. There was a lustre in Martin's face—a pale unearthly glow that I had never noticed before and I was suddenly captivated by his presence. Looking as though he were in a trance, he stood up and walked to a nearby flower vendor and, without word of negotiation, obtained an offering. He then turned and slowly proceeded down the steps to the waters of the Ganges. I wasn't the only one captivated by his presence. Where before there had been endless chatter and negotiation, there was now hush—the eyes of all the pilgrims come to make evening puja, the eyes of all the hawkers, the chai vendors and the holy men, they all followed Martin. Maybe the steps were wet from some wayward chop—I don't know, but what happened next I will never forget. Descending towards the water with all the presence of Moses descending to the Red Sea for a parting, Martin suddenly slipped, falling backwards, sending his flailing legs skyward and his *puja* bowl tumbling down the final steps, scattering petals en route. The candle plopped flamelessly into the Ganges.

The scene was so sudden and unexpected that I couldn't help but burst into laughter, but I laughed alone; the surrounding Indians didn't see it as a matter of amusement and Martin was quickly surrounded by helping hands, restoring him carefully to his feet and senses—gestures of heartfelt public concern for a lightly bruised pilgrim that went far beyond those for the dying rickshaw driver earlier in the day.

~~~

Back in Rishikesh, I soon became friendly with and took refuge in Helena, another Rishikesh night bird, who I would repeatedly bump into on my nighttime walks. There was a magnetic openness about her. After some nights, talking on street corners, we began to retire to my room or hers to continue talking in shelter. We soon discovered we had something in common—our attraction to women! Night after night, we would sit wrapped in the same blanket into the wee small hours, talking about girls and relationships in an openhearted flow. She was an attractive woman, of Cuban descent, with a fantastic full figure and steady brown eyes. It all seemed a little surreal—here was a woman looking like my fantasy, sharing my fantasy. The ease with which we shared our tales of sexual encounters seemed to unblock certain communication channels, and our conversation would seamlessly run from tales of day-long lesbian love couplings to matters sublime.

Helena and I were soon joined by Oran, a veritable talking machine that could sound off all night. Oran was a curly-headed Jewish giant. Despite the volume of his talk, it was never for a moment dull. That is what I remember—the sensation of the spell he cast on me listening to him, but nothing of what he talked about—nothing until it became personal that is—for what brought him to us was the great urge to get something off his chest. During his long philosophical monologues, he would suddenly relate what he was saying to his relationship with his fiancé. In these moments, his features became suddenly serious and here, his open expression would suddenly break. I noticed at these breaks he would simultaneously break from physical contact with Helena, be it from holding her hand, or simply leaning against her. Then ensued the only silences we would experience together, poignant, awkward silences, after which Oran would usually begin to talk morally, questioning, for example, whether it was right to be in a bed with a woman at 3 a.m. while engaged to be married to another and then leave— leave Helena and me to drift off curled up beside each other. But Oran was drawn back night after night. It was obvious to me that he had to tell us something and whatever it was that was bothering him, the sooner he got it out the better.

One night after the usual three-hour warm-up monologue, he again breached the topic of his relationship. As he had been talking, Helena had been lying in the middle of us in a happy half snooze and we both had our hands on her back. As on previous nights, after a brief snippet regarding his relationship, he took his hands from Helena's back and went quiet.

'Put your hands back on Helena,' I told him.

'What?' he asked confused.

'Put your hands back on Helena's back and tell me what you

have to tell!'

And so he did. Maintaining his hands on Helena's back, once again his words started to flow, but now there was a new voice, a voice that had been held silent by the mesmerism of his endless talk; now he spoke with his inner voice. He started to tell of his fiancé, of the fear he had of marrying into a violent family. Once again, he broke off from talking, again subconsciously and simultaneously breaking contact with Helena. Now he wanted me to talk about my relationship. I felt suddenly on the spot, awkward, unsure where to begin.

'Put your hands on Helena!' he ordered.

So we both put our hands on Helena's back, and sure enough, I could feel a warmth entering me—a warmth free of judgement, a warmth that was the will simply to heal. I began to talk.

Our sessions continued like this for some nights, Oran and I talking to each other via Helena's body. She was the cathartic wheel of truth, the necessary physical vehicle for its flow. She would usually curl up to sleep between us somewhere around 2 a.m. while Oran and I continued, often until the dawn. While Helena slept like a contented cat, Oran and I would face each other on either side of her, both hands on her back, releasing two rivers of years of unexpressed emotions. Helena was the meeting point of those waters.

The hotel was basically a kind of happy lunatic asylum, populated by those struck by divine madness and those who were just plain mad—I felt right at home! In previous years, I had learned only to close myself. Any statement of my being had aroused my wife's anger—had her screaming that I was an egoist. I had learned to close, close, close, to become invisible. But here these crazy angels saw me, beckoned for my expression and wished to heal me. As I began to heal, I began to tremble. All the time I trembled, trembled as my true self shook its way back to the surface—a self that felt no shame in loving, a self that had long longed only for love.

The trembling continued day after day—my heart opened day after day. Every day, I met someone new and felt as though I were falling in love with someone new. Every day, I met my best friend or a woman who felt like the woman of my dreams. Encounters like I had only rarely experienced in life became a daily occurrence. It didn't make any sense, but I didn't try to make sense of it—just let it happen; something deep inside me knew it needed to happen.

With the trembling was an undercurrent of fear, an inexplicable fear based on no obvious reason, the fear perhaps one experiences 'being in love', the knowledge that I was where I always sought to be and the disappearance of time that accompanies it, the knowledge that there was no longer a better future, there was no 'other' place to yearn for or scurry off to. As I met each new soul, I was presenting myself naked—I was not something else, from somewhere else, becoming something else; I felt like a naked and vulnerable child in the hands of everyone.

The undercurrent of fear gradually mounted day after day.

As my long- erected barriers of cynicism and distrust began to crumble, I feared I was losing myself. I wanted to run to the safety of perspective. This desire drew me once again to the familiar façade of Martin. I found him planning a new, longer two-wheeled adventure—this time a long motorbike ride into the high mountains, ostensibly to pay his respects to a river and some Himalayan peaks which to him were the manifestation of one deity or another. When he told me his plan I instantly dropped all mine and decided to accompany him. Like his deities, the thought of empty Himalayas and white watered river torrents pulled me forcefully.

~~~

For two days, we wound our way gradually upwards along 300 miles of serpentine bends as the road wound its way along the ever-dwindling Ganges, followed it up towards its source in the high Himalayas, the wide, languid sandy shored waters of Rishikesh gradually narrowing to rushing white torrents deep in rocky gorges. As we progressed, the road surface changed from heavily potholed and dusty at lower altitudes to heavily potholed and muddy higher up, slick mud that had our profile-free road tyres skidding all over. The gorges sometimes began directly at the roadside, often with no barrier to separate travellers from the dizzying drops into the torrents below. Indeed, in some parts, the surface had collapsed into the gorge, leaving only a single-track passage squeezed against a precipice. During passes like this, I was grateful to be on a bike and not in a car or bus, which could not have had more than a couple of feet to spare. The riding required all my concentration, leaving no room for romantic ponderings. The further into the mountains we progressed, the clearer my mind became. Once again, I knew I was where I was meant to be.

With the ever-increasing altitude, the towns thinned out, becoming all the while more desolate and shabby in the winter gloom, the residents appearing ever dirtier, probably due to their refraining from washing in the frigid winter waters of recent snowmelt. Stopping to eat biscuits at the outskirts of one mountain village, we were surrounded by a circle of silent, dirty-faced children. Their big eyes stared at us out of frozen mud-caked features, only ever moving to reach out little biscuit-receiving hands from within the bundle of filthy rags that served as clothing.

As we neared the border, most settlements were little more than military garrisons. The ever-dropping temperatures forced us to purchase extra woolly underwear and stuff newspapers down our shirts in an attempt to block out some of the biting wind-chill. Not long after the road became more and more iced up, we skidded our way between tarmac patches as best we could, having many silly accidents that had us full of nervous giggles, proceeding bit by bit until the road resembled something like a wide toboggan piste. When we could ride no further, we abandoned the bikes and proceeded on foot to climb an adjacent mountain, rising directly from the roadside.

Two exhilarating hours later, scrambling onto a high ridge, I was rewarded with possibly the most amazing view of my life. The ridge was like a rocky knife's edge that seemed to run forever upward on both sides. We were standing at its low point; to our right and left, it wound its way upward to peaks of 6,000 and 7,000 metres, peaks whose pristine whiteness now sparkled in the late- afternoon sunshine. Whereas, the southern face we had been climbing was mostly dusty with nothing more than a few shrubs and knots of yellowing grass; in the space of a couple of metres, it transitioned to a snow-covered north face full of deep green pines. In front of us stood one thousand snowy peaks of Tibet. We sat there transfixed until we realised the sun was sinking fast on the horizon, whereby we hurriedly began to scramble down again. As we descended, we noticed a group of figures watching us from the road near where we had left our bike. My adrenaline flowing and my ego pumped from the difficult ascent, I felt sure a hero's welcome awaited us below. On arriving back at the bikes we were promptly arrested by the waiting military police!

The first thing they did was confiscate our camera and delete its entire content. Then they brought us to and incarcerated us in a local tea house! Long they interviewed us on why we happened to be climbing that mountain, didn't we know it was off-limits, that we were in a military border zone? It all amused me to begin with, but after some hours, I was growing weary and wanted to get some sleep. For police they all seemed rather shabbily and randomly attired; after repeated demands for identifications and proofs from us, I finally cracked and demanded the same from them. The chief produced a crumbling piece of paper from his pocket with something written in Hindi on it—just meaningless squiggles to my eyes.

'I don't know what that says,' I told him.

'It says I am police officer,' he informed me.

'But how do I know—how do I know you can arrest us?'

This seemed to throw him and he went for a quick conference with his subordinates, returning triumphantly pointing at his dirty green khaki trousers.

'These policeman trousers!'

After that, our arrest was little more than comic theatre. Unsure how to proceed, they phoned a superior in a nearby garrison to come and deal with us. While we waited for his arrival, we drank chai, made small talk and listened while our captors expounded the merits of English football teams to us (with which these Indian soldiers passing their time in a remote Himalayan outpost had much more familiarity than me). After an hour of this, the superior phoned back to say he was involved in his weekly game of Bridge and would be therefore unable to conduct aforesaid interview—that a letter of apology on our part would be sufficient. Two letters on scrappy pieces of paper recognising our ignorance and the greater wisdom of Indian military intelligence were soon produced. To expedite matters, we encouraged the chief to dictate the crimes we had committed and our heartfelt grievances for the threat to national security that we had so ignorantly posed. We simply scribed and signed. Suitably scolded, we were returned to liberty.

We returned to the shabby guesthouse where we had left our things—a guesthouse opened to us by its winter caretaker. I had set out from Rishikesh with a winter sleeping bag strapped to the bike, but somewhere en route, it had bounced off, probably tumbled into a roadside gorge, leaving me at the mercy of Providence. Providence appeared to materialise in the form of this guesthouse—the only one that wasn't locked up for fifty kilometres—and the two re-assuring wool blankets that covered the bed in my room. On returning at midnight in the piercing cold—a cold that had all the afternoon's rushing mountain streams frozen into deep silence, I discovered one of the blankets to be missing, probably for the use of the caretaker. Once again, I passed a sleepless night, no longer due to pangs of conscience and a turbulent mind, but rather due to the painful throb of cold deep in my body. My only recourse was to curl up in foetus posture, ever-tightening my muscles, trying to crunch a few joules of heat together, fantasising about warm rays of sunshine.

As dawn broke, my body felt stiff as frozen iron. Stumbling around my room, bumping into and tripping over multiple objects, I hurriedly packed in preparation for returning to the relatively balmy airs of Rishikesh and my new beloved friends, who I was already missing. On stepping outside, I was awe-struck by the sight of the surrounding soaring peaks scraping the indigo flushed dawn sky and postponed my plan, scrambling instead up the steep adjacent east-facing ridge, scrambling for the shafts of Himalayan sunrise now perforating the higher pines.

While I deliriously scrambled the largest physical prominences on the planet, Martin sat in his room and Astral Travelled. When I got back, I found him in the same position from where I had been entranced by the dawn mountains a couple of hours earlier. He greeted me with a cheery 'Good morning Martin'!

Such confusion didn't appear to bother Martin, rather, he revelled in it. To him, confusion was a tool to prise off the goggles of history and force him into the infinite potential of now. What Martin and I had in common was the will not to know—the desire to be free from the known. He was the man who would ride a bike to Andromeda if he could get there without too much hassle. Martin knew that he knew nothing and that knowledge alone was too mighty to accept. The fear of the unknown was the fear he endeavoured to confront. In walking the unknown, he had to keep his senses finely tuned at every moment, to rely primarily on his own intuition.

Who is Martin? Who is Simon? What did I know? A month in Rishikesh had left me ready to believe anything. It had left me feeling like my time in Spain had been a previous life. It all felt unreal in a beautiful dreamlike way. Perhaps, I had just been scrambling dawn Himalayas inside Martin's dream. Perhaps I just looked on as Martin lured the illusion of Simon into motion, lured him upward with the promise of warmth and energy.

In the confusion, I forgot my plan to return to Rishikesh that day and ended up passing an enchanted afternoon wandering the forgotten Himalayas in winter sunshine, followed by another nightmare night of fearing I was freezing to death.

His Story
II

It was when he first met her that he understood what it really means to surrender. When he met her, he had been falling in free space—the warrior had annihilated the last ground beneath his feet. He was falling in the unknown, unsure when he would hit the ground and at what speed. It was while he was falling that he had seen the light in her eyes ... and then he was no longer falling—now he was floating. The ground was the light in her eyes, a light that spoke to him of Home. Then he knew, that everything that would happen and everything that could happen would be all right—that he no longer had to do battle. In her presence all was love.

A Butterfly in the World of Illusion

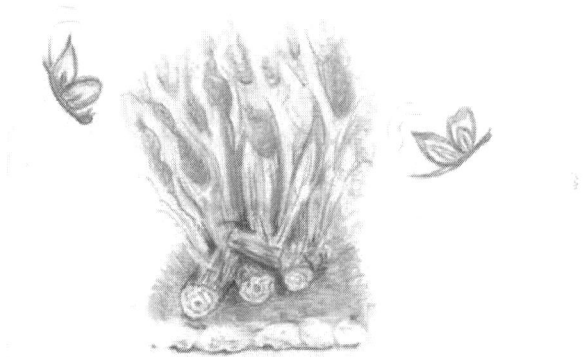

The woman who had been Mara was now Mona, who had been and would be other names, other persons, other assemblages of appendages, was no more accessible, penetrable, than a cool statue in a forgotten garden of a lost continent

—Henry Miller, Sexus

Mami was a little crazy, but in a way that amused and attracted me. Our flights of fantasy were unlimited, even if our daily activities were not. One morning, she might wake me up to ask me if we could go to Guatemala that day. The next morning, she wanted to go somewhere where she could work with fruit trees and vegetables. At that time, we were staying on my small farm in the mountains—what about the garden at the backdoor I had suggested—we could clear some circles for the rhubarb transplants, we could prune the apple trees. She had looked at me offended, "Who do you think I am, your slave?"

When I first met her, she had been fantasising about Helena—telling anyone that would listen that Helena was just teasing her, that she wouldn't really **let her**. Then Helena came on to her at a new year's party and somehow, Mami ended up with me and told Helena in no uncertain terms not to disturb us at night time. Mami was definitely a little crazy and, as I saw it, she was forever tantalised by her lover, a lover who was forever changing appearance—the same lover that was eluding me—and for a while, that lover took my form and mine took the form of Mami.

I first met Mami in the guesthouse courtyard shortly after my return from our Himalayan adventure. I was drinking a ginger lemon honey tea at the time, a beverage that summed up her ingredients. To be with Mami was spicy like ginger—she was burning steadily and she had the constitution to keep burning; she was passionate, loud, voluptuous—she came from a land where the sun beats down mercilessly, a place where neighbourhood disputes could end in tanks and rockets. Mami was bitter about the past, bitter like lemon, all her lovers had disappointed her, had never manifested her soaring inner visions of what love could be, had never managed to cool her searing flames. But she assured me her future was sweet, sweet like honey—full of lovers that would appreciate and understand her. Above all, she was stimulating, stimulating as the tea leaf itself. How strange that, with her, I would briefly come to experience everything I had been searching for. With her I would come to experience ecstasy, an ecstasy ever tinged with tragedy. We would come to discover that what we sought was the same, and yet, that with each other, it could only be fleeting; spicy, bitter, sweet Mami, my ginger lemon honey.

I realised Mami and I would be together when we burned our prayers together. It was shortly before the dawn of a new year. There had been a party and festivities; there had been many around the fire; there had been music . . . and then there was just us—the two with the greatest need, the need to be loved.

It had been a strange night. I had gone to sleep before midnight. I had passed over a month of continual emotional outpouring. As the emotions had poured out, a void had opened within. By new year's eve, I was just empty. Nothing seemed to matter any more. All my wonderful new-found friends would be at the party, but it made no difference to me if I was. I went to bed early and soon fell sound asleep. I woke up around 1 a.m.—my first impression on waking was the certain feeling that this year would be a *year of silence*. I assumed everybody would be in the forest ashram—the party would be in full swing. Mama Amore would be in the courtyard, getting drunk with the Nepali kitchen boys—who would doubtless be joking about her in their language. I decided to go and wish her a happy new year—I felt that more than anyone, she needed a hug. But when I got to the courtyard, I found a party in full swing—everyone was there, everyone except Mama Amore! I went and sat by the bonfire. One by one, people recognised me and came to wish me a happy new year—to give me a hug and ask 'where were you?' I hugged them all, and it was beautiful to do so, but I couldn't answer anyone. I just had nothing to say—nothing—but no one seemed to mind. Maybe the music was too loud, or everyone too drunk to notice. I sat by the fire and the party revolved around it.

From time to time, I watched Mami; she was bouncing up and down, dancing around everyone. Everywhere she danced, faces lit up in smiles, glowed in the reflection of her warmth. There was no doubt about it—she was the soul of the party. She talked to everyone and everyone to her—everyone except me that is. Something in me wished I could have something light and cheery to say, but I didn't.

As the night went on, people started to disappear. Then there was just a circle around the fire and a couple of guitars. Mami was singing some Hebrew songs with an Israeli guy. They looked like two peas in a pod; indeed, everyone in the circle looked to be a couple now. The fire was still burning strong and I couldn't take my eyes off it. I was with the fire.

I was a little surprised when the Israeli guy left on his own. Then there was just Mami, me and the fire. She looked around like she was searching for someone, like she was about to leave, but instead, she sat down and stared silently into the flames. She looked sad and lost. I felt her presence intensely through the fire, but still I had nothing to say. Finally, she started talking.

'Why don't you speak to me, Simon Why?'

Try as I might I couldn´t think of an answer.

'What is it Simon? Tell me!'

'Tell you what?'

'Do you not like Israelis?'

'Do you not like me? Is that it?'

'Did you kill someone, Simon? Is that it? Did you?'

The questions went on in this line, with no hesitation between each— getting ever crazier and Mami sounding ever more desperate. Her presence was that of someone in deep suffering. That presence became all I was aware of and I couldn't speak. Then she began to cry—she cried and cried—and as she cried, her presence relaxed. When she had drained every tear from her body, she just sat and gazed silently at the last flames of the bonfire. I gazed with her—we gazed and gazed; there was nothing in my head—and nothing in hers—I just felt warm and content. Finally, she looked at me.

'What should we do, Simon?'

Now she spoke slowly and evenly, finally giving space for an answer.

'Why don't we burn our prayers?'

I ripped two pages out of my notebook; one I gave to Mami and on the other one I wrote,

To see a butterfly in he world of illusion

I looked at the words that had sprung from my hand and felt a little surprised. Where had that come from? My sub-conscious perhaps, maybe it had emerged from a word that was ever sounding in the background of my mind—Maya! Maya, the woman that walked the streets of Rishikesh, Maya, the name the Indians gave to Illusion, and Maya, the butterfly and hence symbol of transformation. What Mami wrote she did not say. We threw our papers into the flames where they quickly burnt to nothing.

As the first dawn of a new year approached, we sat in silence by the dwindling flames of a bonfire lit in the past one. From time to time our eyes met and gradually I became aware of another fire, one that still burned steadily, the fire that burned inside Mami. A subdued light from the flames of that fire emanated from her eyes. While earlier her mouth had issued a stream of inflamed nonsense that my mind refused to follow, now when I met her silent gaze, the reflected firelight in her eyes held me hypnotised, awoke in me a longing to meet that part of her which I knew to be her essence.

In and out of each other's gaze, we sat there as the bonfire slowly died. The glowing embers became coated in fine silver ash and we put our bare feet on them for a warm massage. We sat and watched while the sun began to light the jungle-clad Himalayan foothills opposite, we watched as it lit the waters of the Ganges below, we sat there as one million birds began their morning chorus and the monkeys started chattering in the trees, we sat there until Spanish Sebastian came out of Mami's nearby room, angrily brandishing his guitar at her.

'You have-ah no respect,' he shouted at her as he stormed off in a huff.

Neither of us felt tired. I felt deeply relaxed—content like everything was OK—everything that had happened, everything that was happening and everything that would. Mami looked like she felt the same. We went for a walk by the Ganges. As we walked, Mami was quiet, it was as though she was resting in quietness after having to talk incessantly half a lifetime. It felt good just to be with her. I took her hand—it felt natural—and physically connected we remained all of the day and all of the night that followed.

~~~

In January, Rishikesh gets cold—not European winter cold—but there, there are no fireplaces, no heaters—and though never freezing, for a couple of months, there is no warmth indoors or out. Pilgrims do not visit in January and most of the western travellers head south to the balmy climes of Goa and Karnataka. When I asked a chai vendor what do the people do here in winter, he had simply answered, '**They get sick.**' A couple of days after new year, I came down with a fever. A clear fluid ran continually from my nose. I began to shiver all the time. I spent most of the day beneath a pair of thick blankets hallucinating.

From within my blanketed cocoon, I had a strong sensation of female presence. That female presence often had a face, a face that was forever changing, changing through the faces of women I knew, through expressions I had witnessed in moments of their high inspiration, in moments of their all-embracing compassion, in moments of their ecstasy. These images were partly from memory but also had a life of their own. Some I had no conscious memory of and yet, they too felt as deeply familiar. While the faces continually changed, the light in the eyes of each remained ever the same, a light which was the fountain of my own hallucinatory bliss.

The hallucinations felt so vividly alive I couldn't tell if they were the cause or effect of my fever. The image of Maya often flitted blissfully in and out of my fevered mind. Even in hallucination, her image had a strong pull on me. After these visions I would scheme on how to grasp her, how to make her mine. The more I did so, the more her image vanished. It had a habit of re-appearing in moments of my surrender, moments when I gave up schemes of how to entice her, moments when the future resumed her native mystery.

Control in any sense appeared to be out of my hands. I had met a woman called Maya who I felt personified divinity. I had even considered that her presence might be the inspiration I sought to realise some of my higher self, enable me to transcend the doubts that plagued me. Yet a couple of weeks later I had come together with Mami, a woman who, while attractive to my physical senses, struck me as most definitely human. In my fever I imagined the source of illusion at work in bringing us together, the hands of Maya! From romancing the divine, I had come to romance the woman. Like a butterfly I had flown from the flower of Maya to the flower of Mami. The butterfly in me had flown from one Maya to the other!

My thoughts fuelled my fever and my fever fuelled my thoughts. I saw Mami as a storm, her winds blew wildly in every direction at once. In the centre of that storm was a calm and shining eye, the eye of the woman Maya. I was caught in the fast-spinning outer extremities of that storm, where I circled helplessly in a frightening vortex. Vaguely I determined I had to get to the centre, remain there eternally if I could. But how? How to tame Maya?

These ongoing lunatic obsessions periodically concerned me, left me fearing for my sanity. Suddenly, I was overcome with the desire to talk to the woman Maya, convinced she held the answers—determined to lay concrete foundations in the magic of her silence. Whereas in her presence, I had remained ever silent and fulfilled; in her absence, I craved to know. The questions I had to ask her and the apparently meaningful things I had to tell her relentlessly bombarded my fevered brain. This need lifted me from my sickbed, and in a delirious state, I sought her out in her ashram.

I found her on the rooftop, practising yoga. On meeting her, I interrupted her session and began to talk nervously of random details in my life, like how I had taken cocaine once and that same day had taken an interest in the stock market! In no time I was rabbiting like a fool about how I had spent months on end in a laboratory, pretending to do research while in fact dealing in stocks. Where this was coming from, I have no idea. I had gone there hoping to put some words to this feeling of deep resonance I felt with her silent presence, but not a word of that came out! Maya listened to me patiently and spoke little. As though warning me, she let me know that, like Knud, in her country she had been diagnosed as schizophrenic. As I left, for the first time, we made an arrangement to meet; we would find an old boat and sail down the Ganges all the way to Varanasi! It was to be the last time I would ever see her.

~~~

During the following days, my fever reached new heights and I remained in bed most of the time. I have vague memories of Mami coming and going—she rarely stayed long—always in a hurry to get something done, like it was always of the utmost importance. One afternoon as I was sitting in the courtyard, drinking a ginger lemon hone, she came by and asked me to help her with a parcel she was posting home. As usual, she was in a hurry. With fever and strange aches assailing my body, it was taking an eternity for me to carry out the simplest tasks. Before I could gather my energy to help her, Scottish Bruce arrived and chivalrously offered to stand in.

I found her an hour later, sitting on the steps outside the courtyard, crying.

"Bruce says you are a selfish bastard!", she let me know straight off.

She sat on the step and sobbed, rocking herself back and forward, mumbling "selfish bastard" to herself—like a mantra—a mantra that gradually took on a Scottish accent.

"Silfish bistirrrd, silfish bistirrd."

I could only stand and watch. I wondered if my fevered hallucinations hadn't been more sane than 'real life'. As I watched, her sobs sporadically broke into strange hiccups. These hiccups then broke into manic laughter, a laughter which soon affected me too. Soon the two of us were sprawled over the steps, laughing hysterically in the afternoon sun. Ten minutes later, we were back at the same table, drinking another ginger lemon honey tea as though none of it had ever happened.

~~~

For a couple of weeks, I tried to heal myself with fasting, with hot liquids, with herbs, with yoga practices, but nothing had any effect. I was keen to spend some healthy time with Mami—to enjoy her company. When she had only a few days left in India, I relented and opted for antibiotics. I went into a shop called the 'The Lucky Pharmacy'. Long had I thought all the symptoms that I should explain to the pharmacist, but as soon as I pointed to my nose and before I managed to speak, he handed me a big pill.

What the hell—I swallowed it. By evening I was cured; the symptoms never returned.

With my health restored I was keen for an excursion with Mami beyond the confines of Rishikesh. We hired a motorbike and set off on the same dusty, potholed road along the Ganges that Martin and I had begun our Himalayan epic on a few weeks earlier. We hadn't managed 30 km before the bike ran out of petrol and we had to flag a lift. After some time, a rickety truck stopped and we loaded the bike on the back.

We got into the small cabin with the driver and his co-pilot. The windscreen was lined with thick coloured tinsels and stickers of Hanuman, the Hindu monkey god. Little metal trinkets and holy symbols hung from the roof on chains and jingled around us, jinglings backed by mantras issuing from the old cassette player. On the dashboard, a cone of incense was burning. The oversized steering wheel would have looked more at home on the deck of a ship and the driver spun it constantly—sometimes over 360 degrees to get round the mountain curves. The co-pilot's sole purpose, it appeared, was to roll joints. We were driving a narrow road full of potholes that often ran along an abyss. With the stoned driver's vision restricted by a jungle–thick foliage of decoration, it might have been cause for concern, but he and his 'roller' (neither of whom spoke English) remained so calm that it affected us. Squeezed together in a smoky cabin, slowly we wound our way deeper into the Himalayas in a happy trance. An hour or so it took us to cover twenty kilometres, where they dropped us at a petrol station.

With the bike re-fuelled, we decided to head for a mountain we had seen from the lorry, a mountain with a small white temple on the peak. We rode up until the road became a mere donkey track and we had to abandon the bike. For a couple of hours, we ascended a tiny walking path, through paddy fields and a couple of mud-brick villages to a happy chorus of 'Namaste' from little children. Up we went, scrambling for a ridge where a panorama of the high Himalayas opened out. We followed the ridge to the small white temple at the summit. Just outside the temple, there was a freshly beheaded goat, its blood still soaking into the dry earth around it.

Inside the temple a funky-looking baba was officiating ceremonies. He had big fuzzy dark hair and a big fuzzy dark beard of the same length—his skull surrounded by a big even fuzzy corona. He had a big pair of dark glasses and a funky smile. He handled some rosary beads like a DJ might handle his decks. He drew his finger across his lips to let us know he was in silence, then gestured to his ring finger to ask if we were married. No, we weren't. So he got out two tiny red strings and tied one around each of our right wrists and then gave us a funky nod as if to say, 'Well, you are, now'. We gave him some rupees and headed back down the mountain. En route, we passed four sweating men carrying the headless goat corpse, the blood still slowly oozing from its neck.

We were back in Rishikesh by nightfall as Mami had to leave for Israel in the morning. As with our first night together, we stayed awake right through, not wanting to lose a minute. It was

Mami's human qualities that drew me to her, in a town full of would-be saints, her honesty regarding her failings, her ability to laugh at herself—and me—had only caused my affection to grow day after day. Around Mami, my own failings were simply cause for laughter, enabling me to distance myself from them. All night we talked about our lives at home, drifting in and out of a silent loving embrace. It was beautiful—I didn't want it to end.

At 5 a.m. she had to get somehow to the train station. It was hard to leave the room knowing she wouldn't return, that we might never meet again. As we went outside into the starlit night, I felt lost. A little puppy came running over to us. I had seen him before—playing with the boys who lived in a hut in the garden. He was so happy to see us that I quickly forgot my concerns. He wagged his tail so enthusiastically that the rest of his body swung with it— his eyes were shining playful joy. He followed us down to the quiet street, happily nipping his little teeth at our ankles, feeling more like tickles than bites. He seemed like a little gift sent to bring lightness to our parting.

Once we had found a motor rickshaw, our minds came back to separation. Absorbed in our parting embrace as we were, we forgot about the puppy and failed to notice when he decided to take a nap, curling up by the back wheel of the rickshaw. Mami then stepped into the backseat, whereupon the driver revved the motor and the rickshaw roared into motion. As the roar of the motor faded, it was replaced by a terrible yelping. My last image of Mami was a horrified expression looking out the back window of the disappearing rickshaw. They had driven over the puppy.

~~~

With Mami gone, there wasn't much reason to stay in Rishikesh. Knud had left a few weeks previous—left for Thailand, he wanted to be somewhere clean and warm, where things functioned as the guide books promised. He had asked me to go with him, but I declined instantly; I had been once before and felt like a fish out of water. Helena too was gone, had set off on an eight-day train and ferry journey to some remote islands in the Indian ocean—as she put it, she had to see some girls in bikini.

Maya too, was gone, had left town without warning me and I was left pondering the symbolism of it all. Had the Powers that Be compassionately observing my endless ignorance sent me a not-so-cryptic symbol? Each time I saw a butterfly, it would briefly bring me to her, or better said, to that feeling I had in her presence—something like a brief awakening of my heart, a feeling of being something more than this physical body.

Mama Amore was still around though and she invited me to her room for a reading of her novel. The week before, she had offered to reveal great *tantric* secrets in her room to Helena and me—and to go to her room had become a dare that neither of us had the courage for. The week before that she had been tempting us to her room with promises of late night teas, biscuits, Indian crisps and fruit—and considering that every shop and restaurant in the holy town shut around 9 p.m., I had often considered it during my late-night wanderings, but always decided against, concerned about how to politely extricate myself if need be.

Alone now, my friends all gone, curiosity finally got the better of me and I went for the reading.

Mama greeted me as though she'd been expecting me just then. She asked me to sit down and no sooner had I done so than she started to read aloud from a loose manuscript. I was surprised to discover it was well written—colourful, graphic . . . alive. It opened with her losing her virginity sprawled over a rock in the midday sun on a beach in Ibiza—'a long time ago of course, when Ibiza was still paradise'—to a man who looked like Jesus.

She continued to read excerpts from different stages of the thick manuscript. Each excerpt spoke of a different man, a different location . . . and the same activity. It all read like the editorial section of a pornographic magazine, a stylish and highly literate editorial. It was the style itself that caught my attention more than the vivid images of a young woman's sexual quest. Mama also carried a Filofax proving her glorious past. It was full of newspaper clippings of her with her famous politicians, singers and actors, which after the reading, she was only too happy to browse with me. There were some photos of her singing in a band in the sixties. She had also appeared twice in Playboy magazine she told me, the last time was thirty years ago—so popular she was they had asked her back at age forty—but those photos she didn't have with her. Then she told me the obvious.

'I'm desperate for cock. I don't know what to do.'

She said it to me casually, as though she was merely asking for advice. I felt for her—she looked deflated.

I'd noticed her flirting in the restaurant a few times. This mainly involved name dropping and mentioning the Playboy experiences, but never with anyone over thirty.

'Maybe you should lie about your age,' I told her.

'You could be right,' she told me.

I thanked her for the insights into her life and left. The time had come to get out of Rishikesh.

His Story

III

When they discovered she was pregnant, he knew, he knew the time had finally arrived to find Home. So they decided to search for Home together with open eyes and hearts. They had little idea of what Home looked like, but felt sure they would recognise it when they found it. They decided to search by bicycle that they might see the flowers of every valley, that they might smell them and smell the coming rains too, that they might feel the air on their faces, the salty coastal airs, the earthy airs of the forest and the clear airs of the high mountains, so that they would travel slow enough to notice the trees and the shrubs, the herbs and the fungi that grew there, so that they might approach softly the resident animal souls. They decided to bring a small tent, so that each evening they might sleep on the earth.

They began by pedalling into the far North, to the great fjords and vast forests. For a month they pedalled in an endless summer day. They rode along deserted shorelines, up and down pine-clad mountains, past silent shimmering lakes, through long rough'hewn tunnels, through the fragile green pastures of frontier farmers and finally to a land of blue glacier and dark rock. For company there were otters, squirrels, gulls, eagles, *deer and elk. This was a virgin landscape—lightly touched by the manipulative mania of man. At night, they slept next to water—by streams and lakes, by waterfalls and fjords. They gathered berries, mushrooms and wild herbs to cook with rice on a small stove.*

Most of the houses they passed on their journey were simple wood cabins in the forests, usually by small lakes. A deep enchanting silence surrounded them, and they wondered 'could it be here?' but by mid-August, the darkness was creeping back into the nights and with it, a chilling warning of the depth winter can reach in these latitudes. With the first signs of autumn, their occupants were scurrying back to the huddling warmth of urban community—these cabins were summer-only residences. The baby was expected to arrive in deep winter. Within one day's ride of the northern limits of land, they turned south—through the endless moss-floored forest of the interior and the quickest route back towards the temperate heart of the continent.

Her stomach was beginning to bulge now and yet, unaccustomed to long journeys by bicycle as she was, day after day, she journeyed without complaint. As the swelling in her stomach steadily grew, so too as he watched her, the swelling in his heart. Slowly they made their way south with open eyes. A long winding journey following little more than instinct brought them over plains and great rivers, through cities steeped in culture and fields laden with harvest.

Fate decreed that one autumn evening they were travelling along a verdant strip on the coastal side of some steep mountains. In darkness, they followed a quiet dirt lane to find a resting place. During the night, there was a recurrent noise of rushing air and water, like the breathing of some immense creature. They woke in the morning to find themselves close to some small ocean cliffs, surrounded by blow-holes ejecting fountains of seawater which sparkled in the morning sun. Inland mists were rising from the waking forests, above which soared a range of steep, rugged snow-topped peaks. The salty air and the barren green coastal headlands reminded him of his Celtic birth land. There was a presence of magic. They knew they were close.

They soon found two nearby living options. There was a luxury tourist apartment on the edge of an old port town to be rented cheap in the off-season months. It had three spacious bedrooms and was opulently furnished. It had a large terrace overlooking the beach below. It had a barbecue area, a garage, and neighbours in four directions. The second option was a half-restored stone cabin in a small meadow opening in an old chestnut forest on the slopes of the mountains. The water came from a nearby stream and the little light from one small solar panel. There was an open fireplace inside, but otherwise, no source of heat. It was a twenty minutes walk from the nearest road.   The   main   sound was the light clanging of many-pitched bells, which emanated from free-grazing mountain cows wandering different parts of the forest—a sound mingled with birdsong and the occasional barking deer. All the land around was public—they would be free to wander where they chose. The nearest neighbour was two kilometres away.

The baby was beginning to press limbs against the skin that separated it from the outside world—time itself was pressing. They had to choose quickly, and in their haste, they chose the luxury apartment, a romantic mountain cabin could wait until they were ready—they had to be sensible, think of the baby— but when they informed the apartment landlord of their intentions, he told them that it was no longer available—the 'wife' had decided against renting he informed them. It seems the Voice of Fear had spoken through them, but a higher intelligence spoke through the landlord. Without any further consideration they bought the cabin in the mountain forest and set about restoring it.

Of Varanasi and the Butcher's Table

Das Ewig Weibliche Zieht Uns Hinan
The eternal feminine draws us on
—Goethe, Faust I

Maya, Maya, Maya . . . and Mami! It was making me dizzy. I felt I had been in Rishikesh too long, a town where all possibilities are nurtured, a town where all flights of fantasy are encouraged, a town without a shred of cynicism.

I received an email from Danny to tell me he was in Varanasi and hoping to spend some time together. A return to something familiar - fantastic! Without a second thought I went to a travel agent and bought a ticket for the overnight train. Indeed, Danny was part of the reason I had come to India and so far I had only met with him for one short evening in Delhi. The thought of once again travelling with him excited me, comforted me even, a nostalgic kind of comfort that is, the comfort of the 'devil you know' a devil I should have known to be the most unreliable cunt on the planet.

As soon as I got off the train in Varanasi, I rang him, but his phone was out of service, so, full of anticipation, I went to an internet café, but found no email either. Only some days later would he write me a brief message that actually he was in Goa with Natya, some 2,000 km to the south. It was raining in Varanasi, he wrote, as though that explained everything.

As with Delhi, I was once again alone and completely at a loss for what to do, this time in the city said to be the oldest in the world, a city where devout Hindus come to die, hoping to gaze upon their beloved Ganges as the soul departs, the city of death and celebration of the liberation of death. An ill-considered destination perhaps for one hoping to return to some sort of normality, but then no destination on my journey was ever well considered.

I passed a few days feeling uneasy. There had been some freak rains the days before I arrived which had raised the level of the city's ancient sewage network, depositing its contents on the streets. The labyrinth of medieval alleyways which constituted the old city were all paved with a mass of brown sticky filth. To go anywhere was to walk through it.

I spent my days walking along the riverside ghats. There at least, it was less claustrophobic and the riverbank walkways had been washed relatively clean by the receding river. Amidst burning corpses and never-ending funeral processions, boys flew kites and men lovingly hand lather buffaloes with soap, half-naked saddhus with tridents smoked hashish laden chillums while encircled by serious men in shirt and tie awaiting their pearls of wisdom, mischievous children wheedled rupees out of tourists and endless hordes made offerings of flowers and candle and incense to the hideously polluted waters of the river they considered holy, where from time to time a recognisable part of charred human body floated by. Yet despite the constant reminders of death, the atmosphere could not be described as funereal, music and laughter abounded and in truth, it felt more like a carnival.

I walked the ghats at night too, when presence of death was more powerful, when the main source of light was the ever-burning pyres and corpses. On the second night, around 2 a.m., on a particularly deserted stretch of the ghats, I encountered an old Indian woman sitting on the steps at the water's edge. I caught sight of her from a distance; she seemed to be glowing. Her body looked as frail as singed paper, but despite the chill of the winter night time, she wore only a thin white wrap. Her hair too was white, as perfectly white as her wrap and her eyes were huge shining orbs. She was sitting completely motionless, staring into the dark waters of the Ganges. I felt certain she would not see the dawn, and yet her face had a calm serenity that moved me beyond words. She was completely at peace with death.

During another night time ramble, while passing the lower caste Harijan Ghat, a man beside a lit fire grabbed my arm. He was stinking of whiskey and demanded that I have a drink with him.

No, I told him, I didn't want to drink, whereby he tightened his grip and pointed to the burning corpse beside us:
'That is my father. Now, have a drink with me.'
So I accepted the glass and together we saluted the flaming corpse slowly disintegrating to ash. Hadn't I wanted to drink with him because of his caste he asked. It took me some time to convince him that it was nothing to do with that, that I simply didn't like whiskey. Re-assured, he informed his three brothers that I was a 'good man,' and they came to me one by one to toast their dead father, each time with a shot of cheap whiskey. When I chanced to turn around, I noticed that the fire was casting enormous flickering shadows on the tall walls of the ghats, shadows surrounded by feint firelight - our shadows. That's when I realised that I had been there before.

It had been four years earlier—an unusual destination for a honeymoon it had been—a tiny houseboat floating on the diluted ash of the recent dead—but then my relationship with my wife was anything but usual. It had started full of dark portents and yet, despite seeing them, I knew she held my destiny.

My wife had spent most of the time there unconscious. She had a penchant for Bhang Lassie—a sweet mix of marijuana and curd—that is available for pennies in government-sponsored shops looking like innocuous milk bars. The first night I had partaken also. Half an hour later we had been staggering along the ghats looking for the houseboat, suspecting that wherever we laid our heads, they were going to rest for a long time. On the boat, she had passed out quickly, but my mind was wide awake.

She had been leaving for Europe in a few days—our time together was short and I craved to be connected with her in every way possible. I had sat beside her all night, hoping she would wake, that I might just look into her eyes. I couldn't imagine time without her presence. Beyond her departure, my imagination was void—it was as though I had to live everything of importance in the next three days.

I had prayed for her to wake—I often spoke her name—but my prayers and my words went unanswered. Sitting beside her for three nights, I had watched the ghats. As the night went on, less and less pilgrims had come to offer *puja* to the holy waters, long gone were the tourists and the hawkers—but the burning dead remained all night and the flames of the pyres cast our shadows on the tall ancient walls that backed the steps to the water's edge. Our shadows were enormous and silently they flickered over this hushed screen, now subtle, now sharply defined, a strange pantomime from which my eyes could not stray, a pantomime that seemed to speak the secret symbols of eternity, symbols which my mind could make no sense of. As I had watched, I had known everything, but there was no language capable of recording it—this was a play of truth and to grasp at it would have been to kill its living essence.

That was all four years before; back then, any future without my wife was unimaginable. I had cast off my past—talked and acted like it was of another person, someone I felt vaguely ashamed of, someone unworthy to be with the Goddess that I saw in her—and in the four intervening years, I had spent almost every moment with her. I had given up my homeland, friends and a successful business to start again, to start a new life with pure intentions—and that had lead us to a lonely cabin in the mountains of Spain—but as I stood toasting a dead father with cheap whiskey, my flickering shadow on the same walls of the same ghats provoked in me the exact sensation I had had sitting sleep-deprived on the deck of that houseboat – the knowledge of life's uncontrollable and fragile nature. My wife and I had come to live a nightmare rather than a dream; alone in the wilderness, desire and jealously had run rampant among phantoms, among pasts reconstructed according to current fears and according to probable futures projected from the same. It had left me once again with the same deeply homeless feeling.

Suddenly Varanasi seemed dark and threatening. Everywhere I went, I was reminded of her and how I had felt about her the first time I was there. The filth everywhere and my loneliness seemed to be mocking the dreams I had once had. I felt as though the memories were suffocating me, similar to how I felt in Paharganj. There, salvation had come through pedalling a rickshaw. So I decided once again to try to pedal my way out of despair, to pedal into the unknown, to pedal to exhaustion, to pedal until it all dissolved.

The next morning, I bought a 'Hero' bicycle, a single-speed, iron-framed dinosaur, it weighed a ton. The handlebars bent backwards towards a huge spring-cushioned saddle—to ride it, one had to sit up straight. Other than the colour, I couldn't tell any difference with the one my great-uncle Willy had bought in Ireland sixty years ago. Actually, it was fresh off the production line. In India, despite having more commuting cyclists than all Europe combined, bike technology is sixty years behind. Nimble and speedy it certainly wasn't, but it did at least have a certain antiquarian elegance. I strapped my rucksack to the large pannier rack and cycled eastward, with the vague intention of making it to Bhodgaya in some days, the town famous for being the location of Buddha's enlightenment. It was to become a nightmare journey.

It took a long time to ride out of Varanasi. The roads were chaotic and all the signs in Hindi script. I made my way vaguely eastward using the sun for directions. It was a couple of hours before I reached the highway heading east—it was hideous. The traffic consisted of an unbroken chain of old lorries pumping thick fumes of low-grade fuel. As they moved, they kicked up thick clouds of dust, so thick that I could see no further than 20 m in any direction; besides the traffic, all I could see were the metres of wasteland at the roadside, a wasteland of mud and plastic bags, of oil spills and lumps of rusting bodywork. On top of this, the road surface was continually potholed; as my heavy rigid Hero thumped through them time and again, my wrists soon began to ache. According to my map, there was no alternative road that went east, so I continued like this all afternoon, expecting all the time to ride out into clear air and rural views, but it didn't happen.

Just before dusk, I took a room in a truckers' guesthouse. When I looked in the mirror, I realised that my face was covered in a black oil residue and I had to scrub for fifteen minutes to get it off. In the room, there must have been fifty mosquitoes and the sheets were filthy, but compared to the accommodation I would have the following night, it was a haven of comfort and security.

I awoke in the morning with no appetite for continuing. I took a walk around the town to look for some breakfast. The dust hung like a dirty dry mist. The air itself seemed ancient and filthy as though no breeze had ever blown there - to breathe alone was to inhale dust. The breads and fruits for sale in the wooden carts at the roadside were covered in a layer of it. The alternatives were biscuits and crisps from faded yellowing packages. I had no appetite for staying either. I went back to the guesthouse, loaded the bike and continued, not drawn to any destination but more in the hope of riding out of the melancholy that was creeping up on me.

I soon crossed the border into Bihar—India's poorest state. Everywhere at the side of the highway, there were people; some squatted in the oily dirt aside tiny kerosene stoves, frying eggs or preparing chai, some tinkered with bits of old motors and scavenged tyres, but for every one working, ten stood and watched, and ten more stood silently staring into space, entranced in worlds beyond my perception. From time to time, I passed rope beds placed at the edge of the busy highway, decked with a tangle of ragged men in deep sleep. Even well outside the towns, the highway was lined with these silent figures. I can only assume they were trying to catch a ride to somewhere and that many had been there for weeks on end. Their ashen faces spoke of those who dare not hope. My heavy single-speed Hero forced me to ride slowly through this eerie gauntlet; the handlebars, bent back close to the saddle, forced me to sit up straight and observe.

Hope itself is a kind of suffering; hope for external circumstances that is. To hope for the world to change is to admit that at some level we are unable to accept *what is*. As I watched face after hungry face standing silently in the wasteland, I never observed any expression of complaint. Maybe there was simply no one to complain to; maybe they just accepted their current condition. My own romantic failings seemed irrelevant in the face of it. No well-titled psychoanalyst could have freed me from my personal worries like these silent souls.

To hope for internal circumstances to change is something else—to genuinely hope for acceptance of what is, is a hope that may be answered in an instant, a hope that is in itself its own cure, whereby, surrounded by what once spoke to us of misery and failure, in an instant we discover the sensation that previously we thought we might have to spend a lifetime building an empire to achieve. And in this moment, the outer world too transforms, our eyes no longer see destruction, but rather the return of materials to their elemental forms, to the building blocks which may be reconstructed according to a higher will.

Sometimes I would catch the look in the eye of a roadside gazer—and for an instant, I would know that physical suffering was not disturbing him or her—that in the absence of an authority to complain to or rebel against, they had looked directly at the pain itself and hence to some degree transcended it. Souls that had earlier challenged me with their lack of possession now seemed light as air. These souls that I had felt helpless to help were helping me.

As the day progressed, I rode into a rural area where the air was no longer filled with dust. The highway was lined by rice paddies, fields of peas, mango and papaya trees. Every hour or so, I would take a break and sit among the greenery and breathe in the rich oxygen. The traffic too thinned out as I passed onto a long toll section of the highway where I often pedalled in a nourishing silence. I pedalled slowly—with no gears and so many kilos of iron beneath me, I had little choice—probably around the average jogging pace. When there was even a small incline, I was reduced to walking pace. Inclines, which fortunately for me, are few and far between on the great plains of Northern India. There are, however, some impressive sandstone hills, which burst out of the flatness like huge carbuncles. They became increasingly present as the setting sun lit them red.

The morning of leaving Varanasi, the few locals I had mentioned my plan to told me I would be crazy to attempt such a journey. Bihar, they assured me, was full of Dacoits—the local name for bandits. When they realised that I would go regardless of their warnings, they had unanimously added one extra piece of advice. 'Don't be on the highway after nightfall.'

As the sky began to drain of its colour, drained it seemed by the surrounding glowing red sandstone hills, the warnings began to echo in my head. Normally, I try not to pay too much attention to such paranoia, but the unanimous agreement on the time and place **not to be** gave it strength, and the fact that I hadn't passed a guest house or any other accommodation in the last hours became a concern. With darkness approaching, my eyes became keener, urgently sizing up the sparse roadside edifices as possible refuges, but nothing appealed. I passed only occasional clay-built dhabas—open-sided buildings serving as eateries—and oil-smeared truck stops offering some mechanical services. As the sun disappeared, the chill of the winter plains quickly permeated my bones. Having no light and it being a moonless night, I had difficulty in seeing the road surface. I decided to stop at the next dhaba and leave the rest to fate.

The next dhaba was a dimly lit place. Five skinny youths stood watching over various bubbling pots and a fat grizzly man sat at a table drinking whiskey. Assuming he was the boss, I asked him if it would be possible to spend the night there. My request provoked a discussion between him and the pot-watchers in Bengali.

'You can sleep on the table in there,' answered one of the youths sullenly, indicating a wooden table behind the eating area. He appeared to be the only one who could speak any English.

For the next couple of hours, I sat on a wooden stool beside the boss. From time to time, travellers pulled in and sat with us. Invariably, they were middle-aged men and invariably, they drank whiskey—the bottles silently emerging from somewhere behind the kitchen area. Invariably, the conversation turned to the 'foreigner'—what the hell was I doing there most likely. I couldn't tell as it was always in Bengali. I only knew it was about me as all the whiskey-bleared eyes were turned on me as they spoke. Only occasionally did they eat—mutton curry swilling in thick oil, served in small oblong silver plates. Then the travellers would take what was left in their bottles and get back into their cars to continue what were surely long journeys.

I sat hoping for the place to close up for the night, that I might curl up in peace on my table, but come midnight, the youths were still standing silently over their bubbling pots and the boss still sitting at his table, watching cars go by or talking to customers. Feeling exhausted from the day's ride I was too tired to care anymore. I laid my sleeping bag out on the table and climbed in. It was only then that I noticed a small black goat tied to one of the table's legs. I stroked his back, his hair was soft and cosy. The warmth of our connection gave me comfort and I felt grateful for his presence. Then I remembered the mutton curry.

I lay there as travellers came and went from the dhaba. Some of them came over to stand above me and silently stare while I pretended to sleep. From time to time, the youth that had spoken English came over to me. Once he came with a broken elastic band and stood in front of me. Staring straight at me, he stretched the band taut and released it, smacking into his open unblinking eye, then repeating into the other eye for good measure. Some time later, he came by with a thick machete-like butcher's knife. As he walked past, he waved it in front of me with a long loose motion of his wrist.

'This is Pinkie,' he let me know in clear English.

After that, sleep was impossible. I lay awake with eyes open, carefully watching anybody who came near me. Sometime in the middle of the night, the little goat began to bleat terribly. It sounded like he was screaming the scream of a being that knows it is soon to meet a violent and meaningless end. For hours on end, he continued to bleat, voicing anguish for both of us. If I was to feel the slice of Pinkie, I was unsure, but the pretty little goat tied to the same table, that he would receive it, I was certain. I continued to stroke his fur, but it was small comfort All night customers came and went; all night the youths stood like ghouls over their big silver bubbling pots. All night I lay wide awake on the table that was most likely used for butchering and prayed for the dawn.

The night seemed to draw on forever. I dared not sleep a wink; it felt as though I were still maintaining the effort of the bike ride that had begun the previous morning, the effort now being to maintain my calm, not start screaming like my desperate companion. When finally I was sure that the sky was changing from black to indigo, I jumped up, packed away my sleeping bag, gave some rupees to one of the youths, still standing over his big silver pot as he had been when I arrived, and pedalled off.

My pace was reduced to crawling, all my limbs were stiff and aching. I could only turn the pedals by force of will, a will to put distance between me and the butcher's table. Towards late morning, as a little warmth crept back into the air, I ducked into a field of peas at the side of the highway and lay down directly on the dirt earth where I immediately fell asleep.

By mid afternoon, I was pedalling through the outskirts of Bhodgaya, feeling relief swelling inside me. Here there would be travellers from all over the world, and more importantly, rooms with doors I might lock, lock the world outside!

His Story

IV

Autumn gradually deepened into winter, the sun's rays no longer warmed and the nights stretched ever wider. The baby could arrive within two months. There was a lot of wood to be collected—he had no choice. He bought a bow saw and an axe in the village below and spent most of the mornings searching fallen branches in the forest, cutting them to a manageable size and carrying them on his shoulder back to the cabin. In the afternoons they collected chestnuts, berries and mushrooms together and prepared them for dinner. At night they worked on building a bicycle-powered generator for a little extra light.

For the first time in many years, it seemed that everything he did had meaning. In the so-called prestigious positions of a society hell-bent on economic progress, work had been something that induced an inexplicable lethargy. Yet here, carrying out the most menial tasks, every step felt light, no matter the kilos on his back. On one level, he had never been so busy, but now, there was no doubt; now his mind was silent as he worked and it all felt effortless. Nor did he want for more company—he had his wife and she meant the world to him. Silently, he would embrace her, standing on the forest's green carpet of deep moss and know that he lacked nothing.

When he did have free time, he would sit on the wooden floor of a nearby ruin. There, he would listen to the patter of rain on the old tiles and watch branches swaying in the wind through the large holes in the walls. He could sit there for hours without wanting anything else. A feeling of well-being grew within. It didn't seem to be dependent on anything—it simply was. The voice of Fear had no channel through which to broadcast. This is it, he felt—this is where journeys begin and end. It felt like Home

Beneath the Banyan

Creation: To create the legend in which I could fit the key which would open her soul

—*Henry Miller, Sexus*

As with Rishikesh, the home of the Yogis, as with Varanasi, the holy city of the Hindus, I had arrived in yet another global pilgrimage centre, this time Bhodgaya, the location of Buddha´s enlightenment. I certainly hadn´t left home planning to visit any of these places. Rishikesh had been chosen due to its proximity to Delhi, Bodhgaya due to its proximity to Varanasi, in both cases I had been looking for the most convenient escape. I had only gone Varanasi due to the erroneous belief that Danny was there awaiting me. A curious trend seemed to be developing. Little did I know then that my path would soon lead me to Jerusalem. After that I would discover place more holy to me than any of them. But more of that later!

Arriving in the outskirts of Bhodgaya, I took a simple room in a Tibetan monastery. Alone in an enclosed space, I began to think about my son. I was alone with his absence—an absence that the closed door only seemed to intensify. It wasn't long before I was back outside, walking around the town.

I went to visit the famous Bodhi tree, under which Buddha had attained enlightenment. The tree lay in the centre of town in a temple complex. The approach to the complex was lined by beggars rattling coins, mothers shaking their underweight babies at me and cripples displaying gaping sores and waving stumps that served as limbs. Among these were 'change wallahs' offering ninety-five single rupee coins for a 100 rupee note, hence facilitating convenient distribution of alms. As I passed, many prostrated to the undoubted rupees that I carried in my pocket.

Entering the fenced-off temple complex, the urban chaos was instantly replaced by great cleanliness and orderliness on a level that I had never before witnessed in India, but the prostration continued. Here, the full-limbed prostrated before the idol and I felt as uncomfortable as I had outside.

As I walked round the tree, a leaf drifted down and I caught it. It looked like the leaf that had mysteriously landed in my palm in the moment I admitted to Knud that my relationship with my wife was over. An Oriental lady who had witnessed the catch, approached me and told me that this was an auspicious sign.

Walking back to my room at dusk I stopped for a chai beneath a large banyan tree, where an old couple had built a simple cooking area and benches from dried mud. Here there were no tourists, no monks, no pilgrims, just some locals coming and going from their daily tasks. I drank sweet chai on a dried mud bench. For the first time in what seemed like an eternity, I started to feel something like rest.

When I woke up the next morning, not knowing what else to do, I went back to the banyan tree chai stand. It was the place that drew me—a neutral space free of the material clamour and need that permeated the streets and marketplace, a need that I sensed too in the Buddha temple, albeit in less material form— both spoke to me of lack and the need to become. Here, the old couple quietly went about their business of simply providing chai. They had built a little circular fireplace in the centre of the bench, which they kept fired by collected bits of wood and twigs, above which they placed a kettle to boil water and a pot to prepare the chai on a tripod grill.

Sitting there, I felt comfort, a feeling that had been completely absent since leaving Rishikesh. After the chai, I ended up staying much longer than I expected, no longer feeling like I should be somewhere else. I finally left to buy a few necessities, but once that was done, I felt drawn back and finally spent most of the day sitting there on the low dried-mud-block bench beneath the dusty banyan tree. From time to time, I ordered chais, but mostly I just sat there as the world went by. This didn't bother the chai vendor and his wife, indeed they barely seemed to recognise my presence.

The next day, I woke up and went there directly. There was a sense of harmony beneath the Banyan, and despite being close to a busy street, the chaos of the street did not seem to enter. Sometimes I watched the old couple. They seldom spoke to each other, yet obviously a deep understanding flowed between them. One might be adding tea leaves to the pot while the other added twigs to the fire. Neither appeared to have a role or particular duty, both simply did what needed to be done. In their silent manner, what this was in any moment appeared to unify them and the two aged bodies synchronised in movement accordingly. Nor did they talk much to the customers—each was treated with the same simple courtesy, welcomed by a simple nod and smile, whether they be a monk in purple robes, a workman in greasy rags, or a tourist with jingling pockets—all were treated the same. The same simple courtesy was always extended to me when I arrived.

I went back the following day also and the next, each day sitting for longer and longer, until my entire days were being spent there and I no longer considered going anywhere else. As time went by, I became aware that passers-by on the street barely recognised my presence—as an obvious Westerner, sitting in public unnoticed in India is a rarity indeed—yet here as the days passed, I seemed to blend into the background as remarkably as an old lamppost. Here, I could sit all day without any disturbance; here, my mind could wander uninterrupted.

Visions of my past drifted into my consciousness and with them, ever-weakening emotions. Plans and hopes for the future often arose too and with them, always a sense of frustration and pointlessness, as though I were being ordered to do something by a boss in whom I had lost my trust. I existed there in a state best described as trance. The old couple, the mud-built fireplace, the workmen, the monks and the families that came and went, they all seemed like part of my imagination—objects that, if I gave them specific attention, would take on a larger sense of reality, which otherwise just blended into an ever-changing kaleidoscope of colour, an ever-changing melody of indifferentiable sound. Hours would pass like this, how many at a stretch I couldn't tell, for I had nothing to do, nowhere to go.

Often contemplated my past—what new was there to live I wondered? I had travelled to all the corners of the earth; I had shared my deepest self with friends and lovers, friends and lovers from every social stratum, religion and continent. I had climbed mountains, surfed waves and pedalled across continents. I had been a farmhand, a lecturer, a sportsman and a businessman, all with reasonable success. There was nothing left that I had ever wanted to 'become', that I hadn't already to some degree.

I also relived my life's failures and disappointments, the rejections, unachieved goals, the disappearance of friends and lovers who had meant the world to me, the disillusionment I had experienced with every hero or ideal that I had gotten close enough to. In a sense everything I never wanted to happen, had happened also and yet here I was, essentially the same as ever.

In my undisturbed state, these contemplations often aroused in me the same emotions and bodily sensations as they had in 'real life'. The 'inner life' which had accompanied them, I relived—only sitting on this mud bank beneath a banyan tree the process of reaching these inner states of being did not require titles, money, the presence of specific people, or any travel in the physical sense. The process no longer required time!

Periodically I would snap out of this—I would jump to my feet with a start, gripped by a sudden fear that I was disappearing from the world, fearing that I was slipping into madness. At these times I usually walked hastily to a nearby internet post, desperately hoping to read news of someone needing me, or maybe a message from Maya that she wanted to meet me somewhere—anywhere! On both counts, I was inevitably disappointed. After these manic escapades, I would always return to sit under the banyan tree—drawn by the thought of a comforting chai—and soon I would slip back into contemplations. Once back there, I usually felt grateful for my inconspicuousness, my non-identity and questioned what it really was that had caused me to leave.

Most of the time I was content with being nobody. Occasionally the other people who came for chai would say a few words. These interactions were rarely more than simple greetings, never did they involve me in schemes, or mention things I should do or see—in short, they didn't disturb me. Others would often sit in silence on the adjacent mud bank long after their chais had been drunk. The chai vendor and his wife never asked anyone to move on or make space for customers, lingering was in no way discouraged. They usually prepared some dal and chapatis for lunch which they would sometimes offer me via hand gestures.

As the days passed, the cycle of dissolving into dreamy reverie followed by jolts of fear about what I was 'becoming' repeated. My sittings grew longer and proportionately, the bolts of fear, when they came, came with a higher voltage—and this finally had its consequences.

The experience I was having was a little like when I had arrived in Rishikesh—having arrived there more by chance than plan, I had also drifted for hours on end. The difference there had been that things had a certain comforting familiarity—on *coming back* from my trances, I had found myself sitting in a restaurant chair in the courtyard of a hotel full of Westerners, with a menu at my fingertips and the belief that I was soon to meet up with my best friend—there, on returning to earth, I fell gently into the safety net of the known. Here I would return to find myself sitting on hardened mud beneath a dusty tree at the roadside. Here, in the poorest state of India, Indians were passing me by without batting an eyelid, as though I had sat there every day of my life, as though I were blending into the background, as though I weren't there!

As in Rishikesh, again it was Knud's words that finally took me out of it; it was the words of my officially-classified schizophrenic buddy that de-railed my astral train. It happened after a particularly long session under the Banyan tree. I had gone there at dawn for a chai and sat all day in calm, watching dreams, dreams about Maya. In my undisturbed imagination, she took on a reality more real than she ever had when I knew her in Rishikesh. Mostly we were together in silence watching the world around us go by—watching as though through the same pair of eyes. Sometimes, the world we watched was Bhodgaya, but we travelled effortlessly through time and space. We rode two Hero bicycles through the Indian countryside, a place where the roads were populated with shepherds, bicycles and animals, where all the eyes we met were shining, where all the faces smiled (a place with little in common with the route I had just ridden). Sometimes I was with her in her homeland and we walked the streets of ancient cities. Others I was guiding her through the mountains of Spain, collecting wild mushrooms and berries. The schism that she perceived in the world no longer existed—my sight was her sight, my thoughts were her thoughts, my feelings were her feelings—there was no longer division. Her presence was my completion and mine hers. Where once she had been surrounded by fearing people locked in separateness, she now moved in the knowledge of union. This separateness that once had haunted her, that had led her to believe that she was ill, in my silent presence, this separateness dissolved. I was her healing and she was mine.

The whole day passed like this, and my experience was that of bliss. When I finally snapped out of it, the sun was setting—the whole day I had drifted in Maya! Anxiously I asked myself 'Who is Maya anyway?' . . . a woman I had barely spoken to, a woman who radiated a beauty and calm I saw as divine, a divinity on whom I sought to lay my burden of desires and dramas. Maya, Maya, Maya!

Gripped by a more urgent panic than before, I ran once again for the internet post, feeling something close to desperation. As I went, I almost demanded of the universe that Maya had sent me some 'tangible' message. I had fallen from the world where belief alone is enough, fallen from the divine to the world of science and litigation—I needed proof! I was shaking as I logged into my email account, but again there was no message from Maya, but there was a mail from Knud!

When did I get to Thailand? he wanted to know—he had been waiting for two months already! He was in paradise he let me know, people were clean and healthy, the beaches pristine and the sunsets to die for . . . and the girls! The girls so pretty and so friendly . .
.

As I read, I looked out the door of the internet post—the sun was disappearing into a bank of airborne dust. Men and women wrapped in old blankets hobbled, staggered or limped around piles of refuse and polluted grey puddles. I could see the wooden cart where I sometimes bought small bowls of chickpeas. Despite being surrounded by cesspools, the vendor only had one small bucket of water for all his sanitary needs. For over a week, I had been sitting on the other side of the road, pondering butterflies and dreaming of Maya—'in illusion' the Voice of Fear whispered, 'it can't go on!' In this moment, my eye caught an advert pasted on the wall for cheap flights to Thailand. Despite being a small provincial Indian town, being a major Buddhist pilgrimage, Bhodgaya had direct flights to Bangkok. I took it as a sign and booked the next available seat.

That night, as I lay in bed unable to sleep, I imagined that most of my life I had been crawling, that I had kept my senses tuned to the earth, eternally seeking that which I might consume. Like a caterpillar seeks fresh leaves, I had sought ever-fresh relationships, recognition and adventure—all to be consumed in the name of Simon—an illusion that accumulated itself over time—someone defined by his baggage, by his restrictions. Would Simon go on weighing himself down until he could no longer move?

I thought about the Buddha. He had sat nearby under a larger and less dusty tree—a tree without a chai wallah! Had he too experienced this continual dissolving and re-emerging? I felt certain he had, but that unlike me, he had overcome all fear of the process—ostensibly, he had lived a purer life than I had, or had worked harder at overcoming his karma. Either way, whatever he dissolved into, whatever re-emerge, the essence of all was purity— there was nothing to fear. He had transcended any label, transcended any limited identity. To himself, he, Prince Gautama, was not the Buddha; Prince Gautama was the vessel that allowed Buddha to be.

The next morning, I pedalled the few kilometres of country road that lead to the airport in the morning sunshine—the air was fresh and clear, the surrounding orchards and rice paddies pristine. There was almost no motorised traffic, the road populated rather with shepherds, cyclists swaying slowly on old Hero bikes and wandering domestic animals. All the eyes I met were shining and the faces smiled.

His Story

V

It was January, but winter had not yet taken its full grip. She walked down the mountain because soon she would give birth. She passed the meadow where the forest broke, opening a view over the long heather-strewn slopes of the mountain. She passed the bend where the young stream babbled playfully . . . skipping and leaping on its journey to the silent depths of oceanic union. She descended the steep trail through the aromatic Eucalyptus trees—walked down to the van in the valley below and drove herself to the hospital 30 km away.

He was in the forest collecting firewood when she rang.

'It's coming today.'

Today? The baby wasn't due for another two weeks! She had just gone for a regular check-up, but the doctor had checked her and told her in no uncertain terms that she would not be returning to the mountain today. He got on his bike and rode to the valley, following the same trail she had walked a couple of hours earlier, then followed the valley ever down, by the darkening waters of the ever-swelling river.

Mother and baby spent the next night in the hospital. They had a bed in a bare clinical room. Nurses came by and took the baby, with no other explanation than 'inspections'. There were tablets to be taken and organs to be monitored. At the earliest possibility, they checked out. As a concession to fearful grandparents, they had promised to spend the first week in a comfortable hotel in the town. But as soon as they walked out of the hospital, they both knew, the only place they wanted to be was home.

They drove from the hospital to the village below the cabin. There, they wrapped the baby in warm blankets and he carried him up the mountain in his arms, carried him up through the aromatic Eucalyptus trees, carried him past the babbling stream, carried him past the meadow where the forest broke giving views over the long heather-strewn slopes of the mountain. He carried him home.

Adventures in Svadhistana

The sun will be in the sky every single day.
You don't need to believe it.
For lies to exist you need to believe in those lies

—*Don Miguel Ruiz*

I had been to Bangkok before, passed through with PJ four years earlier, a deranged few days that had left a bad taste in my mouth, which left me swearing I would never return. Since buying my ticket, I had been coaxing myself that I hadn't given the place a chance—blamed the delirium that befell me on PJ, a delirious companion in a metropolis where the nighttime entertainment is dreamt up by the delirious. This time would be different, I assured myself—I had just visited a bunch of Indian spiritual centres and PJ wasn't in the country—this time would be different!

As the bus shuttled us from the plane to Bangkok terminal, the first word I set my eyes on was a sign that read 'Conn.D'. A rational thinker would logically interpret 'Connection D', but for me, that dot could only represent the letter 'e'. I felt doomed.

In Bodhgaya, when I saw the advert for cheap flights from to Thailand, I had been running from my fears. The flights offered a convenient escape. Actually, I was running from something that I probably needed to face. Although externally it appeared I would be relieved of my concerns—on actually buying the ticket, my internal *dis-ease* had not been in any way relieved.

During my time in Rishikesh, there was a message that I heard repeatedly, heard through the mouths of swamis and madmen. That message was this:

All that exists in the universe also exists within you

In realising this man realises that all he experiences is his own doing, his own creation. To experience this as *our* essential nature is to realise our own infinite potential, our divinity. Man realises that all he perceives is himself.

This infinite potential is something that all of us have experienced at some time, sometimes in short flashes and often during times of deep loss—when a person or situation on which we base our lives suddenly disappears. In these moments, the foundation on which we had based our identity suddenly disintegrates and the whole structure collapses. We are left falling in free space. Having lost our perspective, temporarily we do not distinguish beneficial and detrimental influences—and without these filters in place, we are opened to all possibilities, to all energies—hence, such often seemingly tragic circumstances are also opportunities to recreate ourselves and to free ourselves from our limitations.

Leading up to Bodhgaya, this process had been taking place within me. Despite living 'the good life' according to the best image I knew, our small family had descended into domestic hell. In Rishikesh, I had been overwhelmed by the love and sharing that was possible with strangers, but they had soon dispersed to all points of the globe. My best friend, on whom I had pinned hope, if not for salvation, then at least for entertaining distraction hadn't considered it worth waiting another night to meet me in Varanasi. According to old patterns, I had tried to cycle away from it all, but had merely lurched from one arena of suffering to another. I sat in Bodhgaya under a banyan tree because I had nowhere left to go and nothing left to do; sitting there day after day, I was no longer sure who I was, and thus I had experienced some of my infinite being. Fear of this realisation had sent me running for Thailand, running for Knud's promises of a bright and shiny time in Maya itself. Fear was the seed I had planted in Thailand's tropical soil and it is no surprise to me now that things turned out as I feared.

~~~

I got into the first taxi I saw and asked the driver to take me downtown. Which hotel he wanted to know. In my haste in leaving Bodhgaya, absorbed in the dissolution of my identity as I was, I hadn't given any consideration to the practicalities of accommodation, or even guide books, for that matter.

'Take me to one you recommend—not expensive!'

We drove for half an hour down Bangkok's American-built freeways past endless white apartment-like buildings and neon signs. He dropped me at a large tower-block hotel downtown. It didn't look like my type, but I accepted as it was after midnight and I would be on an overnight train the following evening (or so I believed!). The driver smiled at me after taking the fare.

'Too many lady,' he said before driving off.

After checking in, I took the elevator to my fifth-floor room. It was filled with photos of pretty Thai women, all heavily made-up.

Beneath each was a name in English. There was Sue and there was Lee-Han—one was called Billy. In the sanctuary of my room as I got ready to sleep there was a knock on the door.

'Yes?'

'Sir, would you like lady?'

I should have known it—I'd been dropped in a brothel!

I sent him away and tried to get some sleep—it was the softest bed I'd been in for months. Around 3 a.m., I was woken by knocking again—a different man wanting to know the same thing—'would sir like lady?'

Before drifting back to sleep, I decided to get up early—to sort out my ticket for the overnight train to the south where Knud was waiting.

I woke up the next morning with a determination, thinking only of my onward ticket. I walked out of the hotel without packing, eating or showering— those could wait. I took the first taxi I saw and asked for the train station, determined to have my ticket for the overnight train in my hand as soon as possible. In the enclosed taxi, I quickly relaxed. The journey took some twenty minutes, during which time I zoned out and paid attention to little outside. At the station, they told me the tickets for the night train were sold out, as was the day train, as was tomorrow's day train - and tomorrow's night train! Feeling frustrated, I bought a ticket for the night train in two days. I would go back to the hotel, get my stuff and check out—maybe find a pension somewhere in the old town. I flagged a taxi and got in the back.

'Where to?' the driver asked.

Suddenly it hit me—I had no idea!

'Where to?' he asked louder.

I realised I didn't know the hotel name, nor the street—not even the district in which it was! In my haste to escape I hadn't taken the time to note such trivialities. I couldn't even remember how we'd gotten to the train station—the city all looked pretty much the same to me—wide American-style streets— white block buildings and everywhere neon signs. All I knew was that it was a white tower-block brothel and that it must be far away because it had taken around twenty minutes to get here.

'Umm—that way—I think,' I told the driver.

He drove off in the direction I indicated while I tried to recognise something. As we drove, I tried to explain my predicament to the driver, who only had the most basic English—and me not a word of Thai.

'Big hotel—tall—white.'

'What name?'

'I don't know.'

We drove round for an age, slowing from time to time to scrutinise tall white buildings. The driver was finding it all amusing—with the metre constantly running he could afford to laugh. An hour or so of this left me feeling dizzy and I decided to get out when I discovered the fare on the metre equivalent to the baht I had in my pocket. The district he dropped me looked vaguely familiar. I would continue searching on foot. In a generous gesture, the driver gave me a discount on the fare—some **baht** to pay for local buses if need be.

It was late afternoon by the time I found the hotel. Six hours I had walked, walked under the blazing sun. I found it when I had resigned myself to walking all night—just when I had given up cursing my stupidity and come to see it as a new adventure—right then I stumbled across a nondescript white tower block that might be it. Even looking at it I wasn't sure. It had loomed up like a mirage in the shimmering 40-degree smog. Stumbling into the foyer in a dehydrated daze, I still wasn't sure. It was only when the lift doors opened and I recognised Billy's smiling pixels that I could breathe a sigh of relief. I went straight to my room and got into bed, quickly falling into a delirious slumber.

When I woke up it was dark outside and somebody was knocking at the door. I got out of bed with light and blissful sensations throughout my body. I must have been dreaming something wonderful. Automatically I opened the door to a smiling Thai woman with dark smouldering eyes. She let herself in without a word, undressed and kneeled on the bed as though it were the most natural thing in the world. Spellbound, I went to her.

I kneeled opposite her as though hypnotized. Facing each other, we began to writhe like two enchanted cobras. Gradually our writhings took ever-wider arcs until our skins began to brush lightly on different parts of the body, each touch sending sensations of fine tickling electricity through all my nerve currents. This went on for some minutes, until she lay back on the sheets, still writhing her chest, all the time holding my gaze.

As I entered her, I stayed in my dream but separated from my body. As though from above, I looked on. Where moments ago two purely energetic beings were subtly flowing one to the other, now I watched as two masses of flesh mechanically thrashed their hips at each other. It was as though reality had fragmented. What I was doing and what I was feeling seemed to relate to two different planes of existence. The body worked furiously, trying to pump up some pleasure to the higher being, but the sensory messengers lay dormant and refused to cooperate. From above, it looked like a pointless affair. When she finally moaned, moaned something in Thai that sounded to me like a curse, everything changed. Up until that point, we had been together in perfect silence, but the sound of her voice tore the fine veil of my dream. Suddenly I was transported to another space, a place where she and I played roles and had labels. The word 'prostitute' came to mind, shortly followed by 'sex tourist'. Feeling polluted by my own thoughts, I stopped and sat up.

From the dream, to opening the door, to being naked together, there had been no transition. Paradoxically, it was the moment I had entered her that separation began, but the sensation of dream had continued. The first sound of her voice had woken me from that dream, in that instant I had awoken into another reality, a colder, more cynical place, a place of individual pleasure and individual gain.

She too was sitting up now, her smile now replaced by a cold glare. Just hand her the baht and she would be on her way, thank you. Money in hand, she left without a word, leaving me sitting on the bed.

~~~

I left the hotel with the sunrise—but this time with my possessions and after checking out. My train ticket was for the following night, but I couldn't stomach the thought of another night in Bangkok. I decided to take a bus. If I had to sit up all night, so be it.

The only Thai on the bus south was the waitress. The seats were filled with young Europeans, Americans and Israelis in varying states of inebriation. Many had brought beers and bottles of rum to get them through the journey. An American teen movie played on the screens. A bunch of drunk English guys were shouting at the waitress, something about 'this isn't what we paid for'. I curled up in a ball and prayed no one would talk to me, but I was wide awake, I had remembered what I had been looking for in Asia.

I had remembered the vision of the stone windows. Why it chose this moment to return I can only guess. Perhaps I had to arrive at its antithesis first.

Once again I could see it all—the high wooden beams, the rugged mountains beyond the windows, colourful prayer flags moving with the breeze . . . and above all, the sensation of space, the sensation of peace. The peace that lay within that vision, the peace that I had felt envisioning it in Spain while all around me was condemnation, anger and grief, finding that place of peace had given it all some meaning. Without justification, it had silently spoken to me of the healing of all that had gone wrong there. That place I had visited already in my visions, that place I had believed to be in India—possibly Himachal Pradesh somewhere, that place I had felt was my true home. As time went on in India, I had forgotten about it—I didn't even visit Himachal Pradesh! But was it really in Himachal Pradesh? Visions don't come with map coordinates, so where was it? I wasn't sure. Of one thing I did feel certain—the bus I was sitting on was going in the wrong direction. I began to swell with despair, I had split with the woman who had once been my goddess and my son, the joy of my life, to be here.

How had I forgotten? How had that vision lead me to two nights in a brothel and now this bus ride, sitting across the aisle from a guy wearing a T-shirt with 'Fuck Jesus' written on it. I wasn't on the bus to Hell—I was in Hell! A hell I already knew, a hell where I had already spent a long sentence—a hell I had entered through my own choice and escaped through my own efforts and once again, I had chosen to be there.

We arrived the next morning at our destination—a destination that had been sold as 'paradise' in Bangkok. Rather than a bus station, we were dropped off in a tourist agency. A photograph of a spectacular sunset caught my eye— seen from an island which could be reached by deluxe hovercraft. The caption beneath read 'sunsets to die for'. Knud's words exactly! I had travelled all night, but the story was exactly the same . . . next stop paradise—tickets available here!

I set off to find Knud's hotel on foot in sweltering heat and humidity I could only liken to a sauna. It was around noon when I found it. I felt heavy and drained.

The hotel was on the seafront, set apart a little from the town. Each room had a balcony facing west and I could imagine that, yes, the sunsets must be spectacular. So which was Knud's, I asked in reception. In the garage, they told me! I went to the ground floor garage at the back of the hotel where ten or so modern cars and Jeeps were parked under a concrete roof. There was a door leading off it. I knocked and Knud answered. He looked pale when he greeted me, had an expression more of relief than joy. His room had no windows and a television was on.

'Yes,' he said, no doubt sensing my surprise, 'I have been watching the television for a week now.'

'Actually, I'm quite depressed' he added matter of factly.

In the evening we hired a couple of scooters and used them to visit the nearby beach resort. The majority of faces there were white—the majority Scandinavian families seeking some winter light. There were pizza restaurants, glitzy cafés, banks and endless souvenir trinkets. Everywhere it seemed, accepted credit card. We did little other than stroll between the beach and a café, yet it seemed to require an immense effort on my part. Knud seemed disgusted at the presence of so many of his countrymen and made no effort to subdue it in whisper. When he encountered a Thai on the other hand, he came over shy and humble, taking on all the appearance of a self-effacing saint. We began to share a depraved sense of humour—something that had never been present between us in India, but we were drawn to it like a child's itching finger to a rash. Our laughter was our relief.

Those two nights I took a hut with a tin roof in a family guest house. It was beneath a huge mango tree whose fruits were ripe. Every twenty minutes or so, I was shocked by a loud metallic thud, whereby a sweet mango would be delivered to my doorstep.

~~~

Something in me was growing desperately tired. I had left Asturias to search for an inner peace—a peace that I felt sure lay in the place of my recurrent vision . . . the view of the quiet mountains seen from inside, inside a place of meditation, a place of natural simplicity, a place free from want. The plastic tourist resort where I met Knud, was anything but. When Knud suggested we go to an outlying island where he knew some quiet huts situated on a reef, I marched him straight to the ferry ticket booth.

This time I wasn't disappointed. Three huts were set on the grounds of a Thai family's home, set apart some 200 m down a little dirt path through the jungle. They were constructed mostly of bamboo and thatched with dried palm fronds. They sat on short stilts on the inland edge of a rocky reef that separated the jungle from the sun shimmering waters of the gulf of Thailand.

Each had a small balcony facing the water, each balcony with a hammock and a simple chair. There was a small resort of mostly bamboo construction ten minutes walk away over the reef. Knud's hut was 20 m away from mine, obscured by thick jungle growth. From where my hut stood, I could easily imagine I was on a deserted island. The nearby resort rented kayaks and I was soon doing much of my commuting by water.

I spent the first few days there keeping mostly to myself and reading a lot. Knud too, as ever, read a lot. In Rishikesh, he had often talked reverentially about the books that moved him—all written by philanthropic modern-day saints wishing to bring inner peace and liberation to man. It had moved me to listen to him, moved me to see how obviously he was moved by purity, by goodwill. In his room there, he had kept two shelves full of them, shelves ever lit by burning candles, might any visitor wish to browse his neatly arranged titles. I was amazed more than anything at the *quantity* of books he had there—they alone would have filled to bursting his backpack, leaving no room for clothes and other essentials.

On leaving India, Knud had mailed that library back to Sweden—but being the man of books that he is, he had soon acquired a new one in Thailand. The library Knud maintained in his Thai bamboo hut had the same geometry and all the visual charm of its Indian counterpart—the essential difference being the content, a content I couldn't help feeling somewhat responsible for. In India, the loving way Knud had talked of his literary gurus and saints, I could only relate to how I felt about past lovers. As I had listened to him with curiosity, so too he had listened with curiosity to my tales, which his speech had inspired in me. While his discourses had roamed the domain of the spirit, mine occasionally spilled into a more physical plain. While not prompting this, Knud had quietly indulged my sensual digressions. Now it was me carrying a small 'spiritual library' in my backpack—and during our evening talks on my balcony, Knud who would tell sensual tales, mostly taken directly from books in his new library, books with titles such as 'Butterfly' and 'Around the World in 80 Lays', books of Oriental erotica, set mostly in Thailand—books he was once again encouraging me to read!

Knud looked after me like a clucky aunt. He would arrange the day's activities, organise scooters if need be, decide where and what we would eat. It suited me fine; I didn't have to think much. Sometimes, he would hint that my room could do with a little cleaning here, a little arrangement there—subtle but specific instruction such as 'you know it would be a good day to shake out your bed sheets, leave them hung over the balcony in this breeze for a while'. He was forever leaving little gifts in my hut; I might find a package of fine tea on the table, a new *sarong* on the bed. Sometimes, he would leave a copy of something or other beside my pillow while I was out kayaking, inevitably the theme being 'the erotic traveller in Thailand'. I only dipped briefly into these; it wouldn't take many pages before I would toss them into the corner with a sensation of incipient dementia. Still, Knud would come to my balcony in the evening and read me aloud some of his favourite passages. These readings were usually followed by a pregnant silence—time for me to digest maybe—a silence Knud would break. Maybe these books were destroying some last resistance in his mind . . . he would often follow the readings with sublime discourses, rebellious discourses, fearless words spoken within the frame of his own life, with a disregard for political correctness and the opinion of others that was truly impressive. At these times, he would speak, referring to himself, of the fears I had of who 'I' was, a fear Knud did not repress in himself but dealt with directly in front of me and anyone else who happened to be in earshot. This was the brave and mighty Knud. Other times, the sequence of erotic readings and silence was followed by a lame voice—something like a sheep bleating, when he would suggest we go to a 'girly bar' on his scooter.

I usually tried to convince Knud to go to a girly bar on his own, but as the days passed, he became more insistent that I go with him, often pouting like a huffy child, whose parents haven't come through with the promised goods. I **wanted to want** to go with him—his heart was obviously set on it. Maybe it could be something wonderful for him—and if it weren't, at least he would see through his illusions and leave me in peace.

One evening as Knud was preparing for another reading of 'Butterfly', a passage that I had to hear, I cracked. I couldn't bear the thought of sitting all night on the balcony while he gargled his way through another puerile fantasy.

'Let's go,' I said.

'Go where?' Knud asked like he'd no idea.

'To a girly bar.'

'You want to go to a girly bar?' he said shocked, his eyes wide—he looked electrified.

'Wait . . . got to . . . got to get ready,' he stammered and before I could respond, ran off to his hut.

Knud was gone a long time, so long that I almost forgot our plan. The sun was sinking over the ocean and the water seemed intensely alive. From inside my wooden hut, all I could see was water through both windows. The jungle behind was now in deep throng. A very romantic place indeed—a difficult place to be single, to see so much beauty and not to share it. For the first time in weeks, I thought of Mami. Wouldn't it be amazing to be here with Mami!

Yes it would—of that I was certain—and the thought of it began to grip me like the Yellow Fever was gripping Knud. I had to see her again!

Normally when Knud rode the scooter, he did so like a cautious old woman—sitting up straight, immobile, somewhere around pedal cycle speed. With the 'girly bar' as destination, he was a man transformed! As we scooted down the narrow roads through the jungle, he deliberately weaved from one side of the road to the other—often riding full throttle—he even tried to pop some wheelies, all the time laughing like a maniac. We began to race each other—through the coconut groves, along the beachfront, over the dark jungle-clad hill. I began to laugh like a maniac too—we were soaring! Briefly, of all concerns, of all thoughts, we were free.

The fun ended when we pulled up at Knud's chosen girly bar. We drove right up to the bar itself. By now, it was dark and we had our headlights on. A couple of bar girls came forward to see who it was, trying to squint at us through the headlights. I looked at Knud—his eyes were like saucers. Despite being in the shadow, he was the one looking like a stunned rabbit caught in the headlights. Suddenly, I felt deflated and I knew I couldn't go through with it.

'Hey, Knud, I'm going to head back.'

He turned to me horrified, 'What? What do you mean? Back where?'

I had delivered him to the doorstep. I felt my duty was done.

'You go in Knud. I'm sorry. I'm not in the mood.'

At this he visibly stiffened. 'Then We will go back.', he said, emphasizing 'we' like a dagger.

For the ride back, Knud's features and limbs returned to their familiar deep freeze—he rode even slower than normal and it was an effort for me to keep that pace. It was quite obvious that I was persona non grata—so I rode ahead in undisturbed contemplation. I realised that my time in Thailand was coming to an end and with the realisation, I felt relieved. Maybe it hadn't been a mistake coming here—maybe I had to live all again—in order to be certain!

As I rode under a starry sky chopped with palm leaves, I began to think once again of Mami. I stopped in the next village to phone her.

Mami seemed delighted to hear me—her husky voice was vibrant, pulsating, energising. To listen to her took me to another place in myself. She talked about how good the hummus was in Israel, about the friends she had visited this week, that Israeli men were really the most beautiful in the world—I just listened, let her voice run through my body—the vibration of her voice had me hypnotised, what she said was secondary. Then she had to go, had to meet Sharon to talk about a party at the weekend.

'Yalla Simon, bye bye—come to Israel, break into my house and fuck me.'

~~~

I didn't see Knud the following day, but when I got back from kayaking, I noticed the pretty sarong had disappeared from my room, as had the packages of fine tea and the kettle for making it. It seemed my privileges had been withdrawn.

Over the following days, my kayak trips got longer and longer—until I was spending almost the whole day out on the water. I paddled out to uninhabited offshore islands, where I would take naps in the shade of a palm tree on some deserted beach. I paddled beneath the cliffs, occasionally ducking into their caves. In the deeper waters, dolphins would sometimes leap nearby and I would often pass beautiful turtles heading out into the channel, slowly paddling their short front legs—the frozen features of their observing heads sticking up over the surface. I paddled over shallow reefs where, if the water was still enough, I could clearly watch an aquatic safari. There were fish of every colour in the rainbow, in an endless variety of shapes—flat fish, round fish, prickly fish, long eels, mantas, huge shoals of tiny sprats, solitary slow-lugging monsters and fish that looked like small sharks (and maybe were!). Unable to classify them, I would just float above, somewhat mesmerised, while they swam in a variety of styles between the equally colourful corals and great spiky urchins.

From time to time, I would feel like I was in Paradise—and yet this was Thailand too! I would paddle past the beach resorts that had made me so ill at ease. Seen from out on the water, they were just minor inoffensive blips on a coast that mainly consisted of pristine jungle and white sand beach. All this *discovery* coming after I had booked my onward ticket! I had come once again to experience the Thailand I expected, the Thailand of hollowness, of plastic tourism and prostitution—and now that I had given up on it, Thailand had revealed another side to me, a side that was not a creation of my pre-conceptions. Each evening as the sun was setting, I would be somewhere out in the ocean, watching the water around me change colour, change form even—to something more ungraspable than water, to a mass of flowing lights, lights that were forever bending, undulating, warping. Sunsets to die for indeed!

In the evenings, when I inevitably crossed paths with Knud, he would quickly get onto a rant about 'Yoga People'. According to him, they had 'lost their fucking head and body . . . Will somebody please put a stick up their serious ass. Yoga for the body is fine, trying to DO spirituality—when will they realise that they are it?'

'*Be*! *Be Be*!' he shouted fervently at his invisible congregation, 'like Shakespeare said, "We are just a tale being told by an idiot."'

These brief, electric sermons entertained me no end, but Knud had a grudge to bear and my entertainment, which he soon noticed, was not his intention. So the rants became a little more personal. The following night in a calmer, more offhand manner, he let me know he had been showing his photographs to people at the beach bar in the nearby resort and that *they* had commented that I 'looked like a very closed up and depressive person', and as one had acutely observed, 'obviously a man in crisis', to which Knud himself added confidentially, 'You know you are not the easiest person to be with—so fucking tight!'

I knew there was some truth in what he was saying, my wife had said similar things, the last person I had been cooped up in an isolated space with. Knud and I had seen a lot more of each other over the past weeks than I had planned. Nobody else ever came by our huts. The dirt path from mine lead past Knud's and he knew of all my comings and goings, coming and goings to which he usually requested an explanation, when often I had none.

The more he commented on my failings, the more I shut down—and this only irritated him more. As with my wife and I while sharing an isolated mountain cabin, I had the feeling Knud and I were also projecting our personal fears and failings into each other. The more I shut down, the more Knud opened up—I became the mirror in which he searched his own self-reflection—not only did he project his fears, he also projected his light and he might intersperse his tirades with soft spoken comments like, 'You know I feel connected to you . . . and I am very thankful to have met you and to share with you—you know you are one of a kind. How is it with your son? How is the relationship really?' but before I could answer he would already be downstream in the river of his mind . . . 'You know I go from deep states of bliss over to silent despair where nothing is moving, never knowing what is next, my mind is for sure eroding away. I don't care! I can only do whatever comes up at this moment . . . it's mostly a blessing and sometimes a curse . . . like being lost out on the open sea, enjoying the beautiful endlessness of it all and then realising I'm out here alone'.

When he talked like this it touched me deeply and I knew I was with a compassionate soul.

~~~

When Knud realised I had only a few days left on the island, suddenly there was an urgency to make the big kayak trip we had been vaguely planning together—and a background urgency to heal the wounds that had been building up in our relationship. I took my kayak back to the resort and exchanged it for a tandem—we would attempt to paddle right to the other side of the island, some thirty kilometres away by water and maybe spend the night on the beach there. Knud surprised me by revealing an extensive knowledge of our planned route. He knew of a small offshore island near the north-west tip, which had a lone bar where we could stop for lunch. He told me about some big caves in the cliff-faces we would pass on rounding to the north side that we could paddle into and explore. The danger of our mission, he informed me, was the east coast, where we would surely encounter bigger waves and little possibility of going onshore. While I had been out paddling in no determined direction, riding with the currents of my mind, Knud had visited many dive shops for advice, read guide books, had studied maps and weather forecasts . . .

'For sure we don't want to be caught out there after dark,' he finished somewhat nervously, looking me searchingly in the eye.

As we set out shortly after dawn, Knud went through another of his transformations. There was a steely determination in his eyes that I had never seen before. As we started paddling, I had the feeling he was in deep concentration, but most striking of all, he was quiet! We made good progress, better than I expected. By early afternoon, we were crossing the choppy waters of the open sea, a couple of kilometres off shore, taking the shortest route between the two prominent headlands of the north coast. Rounding the second headland the onshore scenery turned distinctly wild. There, the gentle bays were replaced with rugged sea cliffs topped by thick green jungle. There were no longer any settlements to be seen. As we rounded to the east coast, as Knud had predicted, the swells did indeed lift threateningly, smashing against the cliffs and giant boulders aside us. We dared not lapse our concentration for fear of capsizing. We continued like this for about two hours, never seeing an inhabited settlement or even a beach we might pull ashore. Despite the endless concerns Knud had pestered me with before our departure, now in the heat of battle he was quiet and composed and adding to my own sense of security.

By mid-afternoon I was feeling fatigued, but the large choppy swells allowed us no respite. If one was to break over the kayak, we could be in a tricky situation—the kayak itself might then be taken by the white water and smashed against rock. In wordless communion, we paddled on steadily, all the while paying careful attention to the swells approaching from starboard. I felt as though on autopilot, we had to keep paddling on, we no longer had any choice.

Around four o'clock, the cliffs gave way to a sandy cove, a cove with a little beach resort. As we paddled to the shore, I felt sure we would make a big impression on the tourists sitting slumped in the beach bars. Between Knud and I there was an explosion of giddy relief. We decided to catch a wave and surf in to land. Catch a wave we did, but it soon lifted the back of the kayak and flipped us cartwheeling into shallow water, where we rolled about laughing like fools. As I looked up to the beachfront, half expecting a cheering mass, I realised nobody had batted an eyelid.

For celebration we ordered two beers. No sooner had I taken my first slug when Knud suggested we paddle back to our own huts. Now it was my turn to be concerned. There was less than two hours of daylight left—it had taken us six to get here, albeit with some cave and island detours. The thought of being out there in big swells beneath the cliffs of a deserted coastline at nighttime made me uneasy, but Knud's conviction was such that I quickly agreed. I had the feeling that, on arrival, for the first time, he had seen the plasticity of the resort with my eyes, felt that deflation of a sterile destination after a savage journey.

'If we make it to the calm waters of the west coast by nightfall, we will be fine,' I said, more to re-assure myself than Knud.

We hastily bought some energy drinks and bananas, got back in the kayak and began to paddle hard, my arms now burning with a day's accumulation of lactic acid.

For two hours, we paddled without a word—in the face of necessity my mind went quiet, there was only the motion of the paddle in my hands, a motion that found perfect unison with Knud's. In the absence of doubt, there was no sensation of effort, despite the fact we had been paddling for seven hours. A tiny boat in a vast ocean, the advancement of each paddle stroke was imperceptible—we were carried onward by faith alone. Our advancement in time was only relative to stored images of a sun that had been higher, in space to other forms of cliff face.

As the sun was setting, we were still a couple of hours paddle away from the huts. I was reminded of Knud's final words during our planning session and solemnly prepared myself to calm him, to reassure him. By the time the first stars began to appear, we were rounding the last headland of the north coast, paddling into the pond-like surface of the east—which is when Knud started to laugh, laugh with his whole body, unrestrainedly, a laugh that could only be the laugh of a madman or the laugh of God Himself. Unable to speak or paddle, he laughed like this for five minutes before pausing for a breath

'What Knud? What is so funny?'

'I pissed in the boat' was his reply.

He collapsed into laughter again. His laughter was so forceful that it laid him out flat, his legs sprawled over the sides of the kayak, one foot trailing in the water, his back collapsed on the stern—it was all he could do to hold on to his paddle. He was useless. I paddled alone at the front as the stars intensified, stars that lit up the sometimes rippled water, rippled black water broken by milky splotches, sometimes perfectly calm water, calm water that reflected the heavens and I could imagine we were paddling through outer space. As I paddled us home, from time to time, the sprawled hysterical heap of extra weight at the back gathered itself sufficiently to remind me that it had pissed in the boat and by inference, that the salty brine sloshing around me was more than just seawater.

His Story

VI

When they bought the cabin, they had asked how might the winters be—would there be snow? They weren't so sure about a newborn in snow. No, the agent had told them—not much— maybe one or two days. The first day back in the cabin it began to snow. It snowed and snowed—it snowed most of the time for the next six weeks. He kept the fire burning almost constantly and mother, father, and baby spent most of their time huddled together in front of it, watching the ever-changing theatre of flames.

When the sun came out, they walked through the snowy forests. They carried the baby in a pouch made from a long blanket tied around the chest. In the leaf-bare forest, no longer with any cover to run for, the deer would stare at them from a cautious distance and they often found themselves staring back at the deer. No longer the clanging of cowbells, the cows all wintering in the valley below, no longer birdsong, the birds all migrated—the silence was now intense.

When the spring arrived, they began to gather herbs and berries from the forest. They planted some vegetables of their own. He came to understand how nature provided for all their needs— food, water, fuel and beauty. What was once perceived as basic, taken for granted, now shimmered with a meaning and a worth that titles, trophies and riches never had.

The baby grew to be a boy and the boy grew to be his teacher. He would take delight in finding a fir cone, a beetle in the grass, in watching hens sheltering from the rain under a bench. He would wander off for little backdoor adventures with a red hen tucked quietly under each arm, carry them among the chestnut trees and the crumbling walls. Beauty and wonder were everywhere, in everything—and finally, only in the eye of the beholder. For the child, the world was new and magical—he lent his father the eyes to see, all seeing eyes free of the filters of scepticism and despair.

He continued to sit in the ruin most days. Occasionally, If there were no pressing tasks, he might sit there most of the day. Sometimes he would reflect on his previous life while he sat there—it seemed like a distant dream. Less and less he felt any compulsion to return to 'the world below', a world full of comparison, the world of winners and losers popularly divided according to who had more—more money, more vehicles, more property, more diplomas ... As the lustre of 'more' began to fade, the light of being itself, grew

Reaching for the Sky Just to Surrender

It's hard to hold the hand of anyone
Who is reaching for the sky just to surrender.

- *Leonard Cohen, The Stranger Song*

As in Bangkok, I landed in the Jordanian capital of Amman without a guidebook. Once again, it would be a random taxi driver who would set my fate in motion. Between Mami and I stood the infamous West Bank.

The taxi driver was a grizzly fellow with a fine moustache and a permanent grin that spoke of a man who didn't wish to be anything else. Within a minute I had used up all my Arabic phrases and he all his English. Ever grinning, he smoked as we descended into the heart of the West Bank, listening to a cacophony of Arabic wailings issue from the cassette player. After forty minutes or so, he dropped me at the side of a dusty road, with not a building or vehicle in sight. Mostly through gesticulation, he gave me to understand that this was as far as he went—there would be someone else along to pick me up shortly. He gave me a cup of Arabic coffee from a big flask.

'Kahwa!' he slapped me on the back with a hearty grin.

'Kahwa,' I repeated feebly, trying as best I could not to look as nervous as I felt—and then he was off.

Standing alone on a dusty road in the West Bank, dressed like an Israeli, barely a word of Arabic and hoping to catch a lift to the land of the enemy, my paranoia started to get the better of me. The only images I had of the land where I now stood came from the media (a media that feeds on paranoia to swell viewing statistics and in doing so perpetuates and augments it) and now I was its victim.

I thought about my wife. Already I knew our marriage was over; we both knew—we had said as much, but going to such efforts to visit another woman in a foreign land would surely be the official death ceremony of our relationship. Here I was smothering the last pulse of hope of all that had once blossomed with such promise.

'I will get what I deserve,' I thought to myself—and in that thought, I felt a certain grim comfort—which grew into a detached curiosity - 'Give what I deserve!'. With that another white taxi rumbled down the dusty roadway—piloted by another well-grizzled and happy Palestinian. This one spoke some English. The previous driver had contacted him, he let me know.

'He not going to soldier.' he laughed, before driving me the last ten kilometres to the Israeli border post.

It was close to midnight by the time I found Mami's place—I was exhausted. First it had been a frisking and long interview from young pretty Israeli soldiers . . . 'What did I do?' they demanded accusingly. 'What did Mami do? Why was I visiting her?' I had no sure answer for any of these questions, mumbling my words as I tried to figure it out myself, which only roused their suspicion further. It must have been an hour before they let me go, after searching and studying every morsel in my backpack.

Then it was a bus to Jerusalem, where I was immediately befriended and dined by some students, with an abounding hospitality and welcome completely at odds with their military counterparts. After a lunch of fresh pita bread, rich hummus, black olives and salad, they brought me to the bus station where I could catch a bus north to Petah Tiqwa.

Despite making my way to the front of the bus queue, three buses came and went before I managed to get on. Every time a fresh bus pulled in, the queue converted into a mob heaving at the door. Many of the mob had machine guns slung over their shoulders, young soldiers taking leave I presumed (presume because most were not wearing uniform); there was a bristling aggression that I couldn't bring myself to get tangled in. Couldn't that is, until I realised I would be there all night if I didn't.

I got to Petah Tiqwa by nightfall—when I showed the address to locals, nobody recognised it, not even taxi drivers. I walked round for a couple of hours feeling dizzy and demented. I was tempted to ring Mami—have her come and pick me up—but I had wanted to surprise her, break into her house as she had suggested on the phone—and now after three days of solid travelling, I wasn't going to quit in her backyard. I found a map and studied it long and hard. Finally I found Mami's place; it was actually in an outlying village, about five km to the east. I decided to walk it.

Finding the village under a dusty moonlight wasn't so hard. It was a charming place, a 'Kfar' in local speak—a mishmash of pretty white villas and clapboard shacks, interspersed with orange groves and dirt tracks. There didn't seem to be any order to the addresses and once there, it took me another two hours and a couple of knocked doors to actually find Mami's shack. I finally recognised it by the combination padlock she had on the door—the same padlock she had in Rishikesh, a padlock I knew the code for! Breaking into her house was to be the simplest task of an otherwise daunting mission.

Mami came back around midnight to find me sitting on her porch. She was walking with her head down; she looked like her mind was working furiously. It wasn't till she reached the steps of the porch that she noticed me—her head jolted up and she screamed, jumping backwards two feet.

'Mami,' I said and went to hug her, but she backed off and screamed again.

'Mami,' I repeated and began to laugh—again I went to hug her—again she backed off, this time running into the garden.

'Don't touch me!' were her first words.

I guess when she had told me on the phone to travel halfway round the globe and break into her house it hadn't crossed her mind that I might actually do it. While Mami composed herself I sat on the porch unable to stop smiling. Finally, she looked me in the eye.

'Lucky you didn't turn up last night. I was with another man.'

With that, all the tension fell out of her and we finally embraced.

'Oh Mami,' she said, now I was Mami too. Her voice was warmth. My icy defences that had frozen over during the previous month melted in an instant. The moonlight flickered on us through the gently swaying leaves of the tall palm tree in the garden.

'Mami!'

'Ayy Mami!'

We held each other silently before going inside, where we fell onto our knees, facing each other on the wooden floor. I stared into her eyes—into all the fire, all the passion, into all the dark mystery of the Middle East. Mami tried to speak, but her words were disjointed, chaotic—their futility appeared to frustrate her. Sometimes she would look away nervously.

'Ma ze Mami?' what is it?—she would ask, before returning to gaze into my eyes. We kept staring until she knew words weren't necessary, until a wordless knowing started to flow between us, a profound knowing too immense for words—the place where we stood before each other naked of roles, naked of identity, a place where we couldn't run to the past or future, a place where we were entirely together. I stared at the light in the centre of her dark pupils—I kept staring as the face around that light began to warp into other faces . . . changing, changing, changing, from the erotic to the hideous, from the angelic to the demonic, from the terribly serious to the ridiculous. While this charade went on at the periphery of my vision, I stared at the light in the centre, which stayed ever the same. All of it was Mami, of that I was certain, as certain as I was that all of it was Maya, that all together was the Goddess. Now Mami was gazing at me fixedly too and I knew she was seeing the same in me.

The rocks I had been lugging round in my soul, balls of guilt, regret and concern, these rocks now disintegrated to fine crystals, crystals so fine they seemed to hang in the air and sparkle around us. We embraced and our hands moved over each other's backs, massaging free the last knots of need, swellings of unexercised longing came loose and allowed the lightness of being to resume its natural energising flow. Mami's lips parted and suddenly we were drawn together by an overpowering magnetism. We fell on each other, devoured each other with soft bites and caresses, we twisted each other into contortions without name. Sounds issued from us beyond our control . . . hums, broken meaningless words, short hysteric laughs, orgasmic groans and screams—as though all the faces I had seen in her were singing at once. The song that sang through us was a song older than our physical bodies, a song older than the Christian hymns of my birth land, older even than the Jewish ones of hers, a song older than religion itself. Our song of hums, screams and vibrations issued from eternity in a long forgotten language. This song sang and moved us! Our bodies were merely its amplifiers, an amplification that unified sound and movement. I felt like I was dissolving, my body no longer had its normal dimensions, no longer felt like it had any boundaries; there were limbs and there was Mami and there was Simon, but to whom limbs, movements and sounds belonged was not distinguishable. Doubtless, we screamed out loud also, but it didn't matter. We were in an expanding bubble of bliss, a bliss that had to sing, a bubble of such dimensions that no world existed beyond it.

In bliss we drifted, on bliss we floated, floated until the sirens brought us back into separate bodies—loud wailing sirens that I knew from war movies.

'What is that Mami?'

'It is when the missiles are coming.'

The calm way she told me, I knew she had heard them before. Neither of us moved, there was no bunker for us to run to anyway. I briefly considered dying there. It seemed absurd and somehow fitting. We lay vaguely staring at the ceiling, waiting for whatever came next. As the sirens died down, they were replaced not with explosions of missiles, but rather the hypnotic melancholy of Leonard Cohen's voice which was playing on her music system:

"It's hard to hold the hand of anyone,
Who is reaching for the sky to surrender
Just reaching for the sky just to surrender"

As the melancholy of the song entered me, I realised the transitory nature of our union. If there has been a consistent driving force in my life, it has been the search for my true lover, a lover who has always felt tantalisingly close yet never graspable. That longing itself had drawn me to Mami in the hope I might create of her that lover—and indeed Mami was of that lover, but that lover was much greater than any possibility of *my* creation. The lover I sought may have been Creation Herself—She was an indefineable essence and only revealed Herself to me in moments when I gave up all desire, revealed Herself in the most mysterious of ways. *Her* form was forever changing—I could only recognise *Her* by the stilling of my mind and the simultaneous blossoming of my heart. I recognised *Her* by my own deep vulnerability, by the feeling that comes over me in *Her* presence, a desire to surrender everything I have and everything I am, for all of Simon is only an obstacle to being united with **Her**.

As I lay there, I knew that with Mami I had glimpsed the essence of my true lover, but the words of the song were haunting me. Now that our physical union was ended, rather than experiencing the stilling of my mind, a cloud of tense doubt surrounded me, doubts about the consequences of our relationship. It was obvious that Mami and I were incompatible in too many ways. We would make love again and in doing so, temporarily silence the voice of doubt, but each time we did so, it seemed to shout back louder.

Already I knew our history—a history to be played out in the near future—as we reached together for the sky we might touch it, but from there could only follow free-fall back to the earth. I felt sure Mami was feeling the same. I kept remembering what Helena said in Rishikesh, how she knew Mami and I would come together because Mami needed to be loved and I needed to be loved. How right she was! We were just two damaged beings drawn together to bring each other hope, to share glimpses of our divine purpose. I was Icarus and she was my wings, together we would soar to the heights, together we would fly straight for the sun, all the time knowing the consequences . . . Still, regardless of the knowledge of our fate, we would reach for the sky together if only to touch it for an instant, we would reach for the sky just to surrender.

~~~

It wasn't long before Mami quit her job and we were spending all day exploring the union of our souls through the vessels of our bodies. The subsequent doubts that assailed us during intermissions had us reeling out the door in a manic search for some outer culprit. Occasionally we would visit a nearby supermarket, a labyrinth of commercial products under glaring electrical light, where one million things beckoned for our ownership. Our companions here were other zombies wandering around dazed by the apparent choice our cash and plastic cards afforded us, the choice we laboured week-long for in the name of dubious economic and social progress, labours which enabled us to pay for the car that would transport us along the tarmac artery leading to this commercial heart of utter disjointedness—no different really from any large chain supermarket on the planet. At least that is how it felt to me—to experience spells of unified bliss quickly followed by such disjointed commercial paranoia felt like schizophrenia. It amazed me how quickly my being could jump from one universe to another and identify itself with both. It made me think of Knud and Maya, the officially schizophrenic, two souls whose reverence for purity had moved me. Perhaps they simply refused to act in the theatres of its contrast, to play the role of the hypocrite.

After some days, these brief forays were no longer sufficient to wear out the doubts. It wasn't long before we were off on a whirlwind tour of Israel and Sinai. To the waters we were drawn—the cool choppy waters of the sea of Galilee, to the burning salty waters of the Dead Sea and then to the Red Sea—

all the while running, running, running.

First up was the Sea of Galilee, or the Kineret as Mami called it. En route, as Mami drove, she raved about it, imbued its waters with magical essence and surrounded them with a ring of mystical mountains. Maybe it was just a bad day for the beauty of the Kineret, a grey haze obscured her mystical Golan Heights, from where a cold wind was descending, a wind which deeply ruffled her surface, ruffles which agitated her muddy bottom and mixed it into her waters. As we stood at the edge, Mami was looking to the clear sun-sparkled waters of her shining memories and wanted to know how I saw it. All I saw was a dirty lake and told her so. She seemed to take it personally and I felt a sudden coldness in her attitude to me, 'ungrateful bisstirrd' that I was. Still, Mami was determined to make a day of it, on her own if need be. We drove to a small beach, that was deserted bar three Palestinian women wrapped up in black shawls and headdresses who were quietly taking a picnic. Despite the chill and the presence of these three souls, revealing only their eyes, Mami soon stripped off to her string bikini and strode proudly in. By the time she was in waist-deep, the relentless swells were reaching her shoulders and it wasn't long before one knocked her off her feet and she came up wobbly and spurted out a mouthful. At this, the veiled modesty of the Palestinian girls gave way and they fell about in hysterics amidst their pita bread and fruits.

The next day we were off to the Dead Sea, looking for some hot springs that Mami knew. She had been there before, on some esoteric retreat, something like 'Love in Atlantis'—I got snippets of her memories during the drive. Everyone on the retreat had been naked all the time. Then the men were to stand in the hot spring, cradling the women in their arms beneath the moonlight. All very romantic it sounded to me and all apparently for some high spiritual purpose, (which Mami didn't bother to explain). Mami had gotten upset because the guru, a 'very beautiful man' to Mami's eye, had proceeded to hold another naked lady in his arms. In this atmosphere of free expression, Mami had begun to cry and for the sake of harmony, the guru had passed on his assigned naked lady to another 'cradler' and instead cradled Mami as she sobbed. Now, we were trying to find that same hot spring—and I suppose re-enact another of her shining memories.

The hot spring was in an isolated place, somewhere amongst some reeds and small trees. Unfortunately it had dried up, either that or Mami didn't know where it was and instead, we spent the night camped in the midst of some lukewarm mud.

Our tour ended with two nights of torture in a beach hut we shared with two thousand mosquitoes. It was a surreal place, a deserted beach hut complex by the Gulf of Aqaba. Bombs had exploded there some months previous, the targets being the young Israelis on vacation. Since then nobody went, leaving an eerie kilometres long strip of beach shack ghost town. By day the wind blew, ruffling the waters into twenty marine shades—this backed by the stark red desolate mountains of Saudi Arabia on the other side of the Gulf. In some thousands of shacks, we saw maybe ten guests—and most of these completely wasted on some narcotic or other. Our shack was rented to us by a handsome young Bedouin, who appeared to have a hypnotic charm for Mami. The two of them buzzed around each other like fruit flies, probably viewing each other as culturally forbidden exotic fruit.

Walking along the shore alone, wondering for the one-millionth time, why I had been put on the planet, I decided to go back to Spain, to wait for my son to return. There was a deep discomfort in me; it was now nearly five months since I had seen him. It was a feeling new to me, a feeling like nothing could ease the pain of that absence. I had felt it of utmost importance that I find something deeply meaningful, or be able to give something deeply meaningful to justify that separation, but what had I found? What could I give? In the moment I decided it was over, I suddenly felt overwhelming gratitude for Mami, simply for being with me through it, for drifting beyond the world with me, for her willingness to surrender with me, before something greater than either of us, something we both longed to return to.

Our last excursion was to old Jerusalem, a city whose modest physical dimensions belie the great weight of history it carries. In one brief walk, we passed the Wailing Wall, passed the Dome on the Rock and the Stations of the Cross, the most significant landmarks of Judaism, Islam and Christianity, all piled on top of and woven around each other. The history held so much heavy significance that I could almost feel it weighing down my footsteps. The air itself felt like it had sat there since eternity. It left me feeling strangely hollow.

From time to time, I left little prayers for the happiness of my wife, who had been contacting me in the previous days with ever more desperate-sounding emails; I left some for Mami too, praying that her committed quest for love would be rewarded in some meaningful inner way; I prayed for my son, that he might experience more of the infinite beauty and joy of life, that he might continue to know more than I, that this was the true meaning of life, a meaning that was not inherent in any particular structure. I felt if anywhere, here they had some chance of being answered.

We left the city walls and found the peace of some trees on a little hilltop, the groundedness of an earthen floor where we sat down together to watch the sun setting behind some old windmills. Sitting there quietly with Mami, there was no longer anywhere left for us to go, no more decisions to be made, nothing to do and everything to be. Finally, my mind went quiet, my heart began to open—I felt our coming separation and the preciousness of these last hours together and experienced the deep vulnerability of knowing.

His Story

VII

Just as he began to believe that Peace had arrived forever, his war erupted again. The ruin where he sat exploring inner lights, belonged to the local politician and government funds were soon approved for building a road up to the house. One Spring they began laying concrete in the forest. With the road arrived men with chainsaws. They drove up with trailers, selected trees next to the road—the bigger and healthier the better it seemed—and cut them at the base for firewood. Hunters drove in to shoot the deer and wild boar. Then one day the bulldozers came—they entered their dream-meadow and in a few short hours, devastated the fauna and pushed up a wall. The meadow that once belonged to all and none became ours and theirs, paradise became property.

Then the construction people arrived. They began to restore the ruin where he had sat peacefully—the sound of cow-bells, birds and barking of deer was replaced with cement mixers, hammers and drills. This continued for eight months. They no longer saw animals near the cabin.

During this time, he and his wife began to argue, arguments about seemingly trivial things could run for days on end. Then they couldn't talk to each other anymore— only shout above the drills and hammers. Fault was found in everything, simply because fault was felt.

Strange Birthday Presents

"For some people that look in your eyes seemed dangerous. Women
instinctively knew that a greater woman, Nature herself a Goddess lurked
somewhere in your past and in no way could a man, having known that
immensity be trusted to strive for material well-being or satisfied with the
smallness of the everyday struggle for security. Women knew that this great
mother would call on this kind of man again someday and powerless to resist,
he would be pulled like a bird into migration"
—Martin Prechtel, Secrets of the Talking Jaguar

Emilio entered my life as my dream of peace left it. He entered as the paid hand of nature's destruction. When we first found the cabin, it was in an idyllic glade twenty minutes walk up an old track from the nearest road.

Then I had naively imagined that the virgin nature of the surroundings might protect it from the demented delirium of developers. But to our misfortune, a neighbouring ruin belonged to the local politician. Maybe it was my own words of praise that brought the destruction. When I met the politician for the first time, he had asked why on earth we would want to live there. Drunk on the beauty of the surrounding forests and mountains, I had told him I had travelled the world and never found such beautiful nature. Maybe in my words, he heard only 'property value'. It wasn't long before the council had approved funds to build a concrete road up to the glade—and this artery allowed the poisons of development and progress to flow to us, delivered men with chainsaws, cement mixers and other levers of dementia. That road delivered Emilio.

Emilio had worked on restoring the politician's ruin, a ruin that lay a mere two metres from our cabin. He had worked with an intense untiring energy that was remarkable, ever wielding power tools and operating a cement mixer. From wherever he was, emanated angry grindings, whirrings, scrapings and bangings, where once there had been birdsong and cowbells. He seemed delighted to be there, to do what he was doing. Often when he saw me, he would shout excited greetings. I remember him howling 'It's great to be here—so much peace!', over the noise of the cement mixer.

When the building was restored, Emilio continued to visit. Where once visitors had to pass the healing buffer of a twenty minute walk through virgin forest, Emilio now roared in amidst a cloud of exhaust fumes, arrived with a mind direct from television images.

Returning to Spain from my travels, Emilio was my only visitor. Like an animal crawling to his lair for hibernation, I had hoped to go into a long and deep sleep from the world, where I might dream and dream, until from within that dream I might re-emerge. But the world kept knocking on my door, knocked via Emilio's fist. He came by day after day to remind me that I had promised we would climb a nearby mountain called Fresnidiellu when I got back.

We had attempted the climb shortly before I had left—that had been Emilio's first big climb. Then we had been with another experienced climber, enabling Emilio to climb without being involved in any safety procedure—he had simply been a passenger. On that occasion, we had to abandon the climb within sight of the peak due to falling darkness.

I had no enthusiasm for revenge, 'venganza' as Emilio called it, nor did I feel it a likely outcome with such a novice climber, but Emilio was adamant and kept reminding me that he had been waiting to do it since I left for India. He told me over and over that he had to do it; somehow he related this necessity to the woes of his existence, the lack of love he experienced in his relationship, the financial trap he was caught in—all this, as he told it, made *venganza* on the vast eastern face of Fresnidiellu a necessity. As he talked, his eyes betrayed an inner suffering; sometimes, he would put two fingers to his head like a mock gun. The solution to it all he seemed to plead, lay in the ascent of the 300 m vertical limestone face of Fresnidiellu. I didn't have enough willpower to refuse him.

The day of our planned ascent dawned as ominous as Emilio's tales of woe. Black clouds scudded a frigid April sky. I felt a certain relief knowing that no one in their right mind would climb on such a day. I was a little surprised when Emilio turned up at the doorstep at the appointed hour.

'We can't climb in this,' I let him know bluntly.

We could drive closer to the wall, he informed me, reassess the conditions there, before reminding me with a blank expression, 'tengo que hacerlo' that he had to do it.

So we drove to the base of the mountain. Its towering east face blanked out half the sky from where we stood, a sky that issued a stream of dark clouds in quick succession over the soaring peak, clouds swollen with threat. I suggested Emilio that we go to a safe climbing zone near sea level, a thousand metres below, a zone with short and sheltered routes, routes protected by securely drilled bolts. As I spoke, Emilio was packing his gear for the climb; he appeared oblivious to my words, as oblivious as he appeared to the atmospheric conditions around him—I had the feeling that for him, a more significant storm had long been brewing on the inside and that storm needed to break. I realised, looking at him, I was looking at my own reflection. In that moment, I vividly recalled a scene from a dream I'd had some time before.

Emilio and I had been standing with our mutual friend Pablo, in the same place as we now stood, yet in the dream I had a strong sensation that we were in Hell. Pablo had been asking us how we came to be there and we told him that we had died falling from the Fresnidiellu! We had all laughed. This hell, I had noticed, was an all-male affair—the female energy had been conquered by the male ego. Here, sensitivity and beauty were things to be scorned and dirtied.

The sudden vividness of this memory frightened me and I briefly considered jumping in the car and leaving Emilio where he stood, leave him to work out his karma on his own, but a voice in my head stopped me. All it said was:

'You will get what you deserve!'

Yes! That was it! I would get what I deserved for all the unhappiness I had caused my wife—she too had abandoned her former life to come and live with me on a lonely mountain, she had a child there. Had I really done enough to make it work? Maybe it had been more difficult for her than it had for me. Maybe I could have given her more support? And what about all the people who had shown me love and generosity over my lifetime, love and generosity I had felt unable to return and had therefore walked away from? What about all the friendships, homes and professions offered me that I had refused, I had abandoned over and over because of the vague awareness of a feminine spirit who obsessed me, a spirit with no face or name? Real people I had disappointed and betrayed in the name of a being that existed more in my imagination than anywhere else. For all of them I spoke a short prayer to the mountain:

"Give me what I deserve!".

Surrendered to fate, I followed Emilio up the steep dirt track that lead to the rock face.

By the time we reached the face, the weather looked to be improving; now there were a few bright patches in the sky. I conceded to climbing while assuring Emilio—and myself—that with the first drop of rain we would be abseiling straight down. We put on our harnesses and tied in to the rope. Then I handed Emilio the belay device.

'Para que es eso?' (What's this for?) he asked me.

What is a belay device for? The belay device is the most fundamental piece of equipment in the climbing rack, the device, on Emilio's proper usage of which my life depended, were I to fall during the climb, a device explained to novice climbers in their first minutes of climbing instruction. Standing at the base of 300 m of vertical limestone, I realised my lifeline was in the hands of a complete novice, a novice who seemed to have a death wish to boot. The weather may have been improving, but my confidence was not.

Again I remembered another snippet of the dream—we

men laughing at the waste we had laid to paradise, gloating at our consumption of the feminine, the conscious beauty, a beauty that we might have expanded, but instead we had burnt to dirty fumes in the insatiable flames of our desire. All around, I sensed those intoxicating fumes. Fatalistically assuring myself that I would get what I deserved, I started to climb.

~~~

For me, the greatest draw of rock climbing is not the fantastic views it affords, nor the sense of achievement in reaching some difficult peak, but rather the presence of mind it brings, a presence forced upon climbers by mortal necessity. A lack of concentration up on the wall can be fatal, and even though the concentration required is simple, required it is!

As we climbed, the skies became ever clearer and we passed the most technically challenging section of the route without excessive difficulty. Presence flooded my mind and all the concerns that had been bothering me were put into a new perspective—the perspective of my own mortality! As my mental cobwebs were swept away, a new invigorating mental clarity began to flow. By the time we were halfway up, the clouds in my mind had disappeared like the clouds in the sky around us, which had miraculously turned into an unbroken blue.

Via a series of tiny fissures, holes and scars from water channels in the ever-changing limestone mosaic, we worked our way step by step up the mighty face, the disappearing ground only visible between our feet. For company on the wall, we had some huge and majestic buzzards who would glide past us at close quarters with a loud 'whhhiinnng' emanating from their motionless wings, wings with a span well beyond my height.

Emilio was smiling often now and made jokes as he caught up to me at belay points—he looked to be experiencing the transformation he had sought. We made fast progress and in a few hours, only two rope lengths separated us from the peak.

Then, two hundred and fifty metres up, with only fifty metres left to go, it all started to go hideously wrong. The skies began to darken again, rapidly. We were now in the most vulnerable position we could be on the whole wall, six or so abseils from the ground and time-wise, a similar distance from the peak. With a sense of urgency, we sped up, trying to make the peak from where we would be able to scramble down an easier route on the other side if the heavens were to open. With a mere thirty or so metres remaining, open they did, open with a fury. Sleet began to fall hard and the rock instantly became very slippery, making progress impossible. Our only option was to descend the same route we had just climbed. I set up a belay and waited for Emilio, who as second climber, was carrying a backpack with our spare clothes. When he caught up, I asked him for my rain jacket.

'Lo deje en el suelo.' he told me—he had left it on the ground!

'Que!?'

'Querría quitarnos un poco de peso.' he had wanted to save us some weight!

I set up our emergency abseil as the cold sleet slowly melted through my permeable layers. The towering rock faces around us had blackened like the sky, highlighting the few crevices where the snow had managed to cling on, giving them the aspect of long white spectral fingers reaching downward.

After our first abseil we discovered an unexpected difficulty. The ropes had swollen in the sleet and now jammed in the abseil anchor as we tried to retrieve them. It took our combined effort to budge them, both of us hauling with both hands on the same metre of rope. As we did so, Emilio directed accusing eyes at the sky and howled wild oaths at the powers that had cursed his life, as though the storm and the dire circumstances had been arranged to torture him alone.

Completing the second abseil, I heard a strange croaking noise coming from above. I looked up to see Emilio vomiting from his small rocky perch some forty metres above. Not far above him a bolt of lightning struck the peak.

With the ever jamming ropes, our progress down the wall was little faster than it had been upward. We were now enveloped in cloud and it was difficult to judge how far away the ground was. As our bodies became numb with cold, the ropes swelled further and retrieving them became ever more difficult. After four abseils, it began to look uncertain if we could at all. It took both of us pulling the same rope with all our arm strength and bending over simultaneously to add weight, to budge them the length of a baguette. All the while, Emilio, while not quite vomiting, continued to croak loudly, sounding like a demented bullfrog.

Suddenly it all struck me as preposterous, the situation seemed a parody of all I could ever have imagined going wrong—and I had a strong sensation that none of it was real, that I was just dreaming the whole thing. I half expected Emilio to come falling past me, or to fall myself—it all just didn't feel real! Staring into its eye, death itself didn't seem real, seemed to lose its form and meaning, something like how Mami had disappeared as I had stared fixedly into her eyes and something vaster had emerged. I began to laugh, began to sense the deepest calm I had experienced in months. Despite clinging onto cold hard rock, I had an overriding sensation of softness and embrace. Despite the sleet quickly melting over my body, I had the sensation of warmth. I heard a woman laughing gently nearby, as though it were a loving expression to a newborn. All this and yet I felt entirely present—and in that presence, I sensed the feminine, I sensed purity, I sensed the presence that could only be Her!

In this dreamlike presence, as we descended into the freezing gloom, I felt certain that everything that was happening was guided by some intention higher than my own consciousness, that everything was exactly as it should and had to be. The immortal caressed the mortal; I felt only gratitude to Emilio for dragging me to my Colosseum, where I might confront directly the ferocious beasts of my own conscience—beasts that roamed my mind as remorse, guilt and failure now transformed in threats of free fall, hypothermia and exhaustion, new forms with which I could work directly with my body, with my trust in my technically inept partner Emilio, who had long placed all his trust in my shabby form.

Slowly we descended, the energy of our bodies dwindling with our altitude. Tied by threads physical and ethereal, we made it to the ground as darkness was falling. In silence, we staggered back to the car and drove out of the mountains, stopping half an hour later at the first village to drink a beer.

Under the bright lights, alcohol entering my bloodstream, I began to shiver and then to shake. It was only then I remembered it was my birthday—with all the dramas of the day I hadn't given it any consideration—and how nearly my death day! I told Emilio and we both started to laugh uncontrollably. Emilio was shining and wasted and vibrant. The other people in the bar all looked very orderly by comparison; most were playing cards and I had an overwhelming sensation that they were merely cardboard background.

His Story

VIII

The child would be ignored for hours on end as they shouted at each other about hair in the bath, about a casual phrase written to another woman years ago. Every word spoken became a pretext for an argument, so he spoke less and less. Looking to the other side of the room, she screamed at a demon that he could not see or recognise, a demon that she gave his name. The air around them seemed to be disappearing—the goddess he had fallen in love with seemed to have left. Without her loving gaze, his heart began to close. He became cold and distant. He became afraid to open—afraid to express his love. The love unexpressed turned stagnant inside him, turned vile and malignant.

He looked on in despair, feeling loss, loss of that which was most precious to him. From that loss arose anger. That anger grew into his demon. His demon now took on her appearance, the face that had once been the face of his goddess. When he couldn't bear it anymore, his silence broke and unable to look at her, he too screamed at his demon across the room, a demon he gave her name. The voice that screamed was the Voice of Fear.

This went on for over a year. He worried about the effect it was *having on his wife, on himself, but most of all, on the child. He realised that they had to try to regain perspective, and the only way to do so was to be apart. Individually, they had to seek their own healing to understand the true nature of their demons. They had to be able to look at each other in the eye again and not see them.*

The damage ran deep and he didn't know how to repair it; all he had was a vision of a place, a place that when he imagined it, he still felt peace—he felt his only hope was to find that place.

They left the mountain and she went west with the boy and he went east alone. They kept going until they stood on opposite sides   of   the   planet.

A Year of Silence

In his frenzied love for you he longs to break the chains of his imprisonment—he has no choice

—Rumi

In the weeks before my wife and son returned, the need to make some sense of it all heated in me to boiling point. What on earth had it all been for? Still I didn't know!

With ten days left until their return, I took drastic measures—I stopped eating! It had a certain effect. Rather than wandering off in dizzying plans to fix the world (plans with so many variables that they inevitably drove me to a frightening feeling of vertigo), the constant presence of hunger was strong enough to bring me to my current situation. After five or six days, I also lacked the physical energy to leave the house. Like a convalescent, going nowhere and doing nothing just felt right. As outer substance no longer entered my body, so too the substance of the outer world appeared less solid.

On the tenth day of fasting, my son and wife finally returned. Emilio drove me to meet them at a bus station in a city two hours away. My son had a corduroy jacket, his hair hung over his eyes and he was paler than I remembered, possibly from the long journey. He looked wise and my first impression was that I was in front of a little professor. He held out two small red flowers to me, flowers which had wilted during the journey and now draped over his closed fist. My wife had a glow which surprised me; in the emails she had been sending, her endless accusations had been mixed with a constant stream of personal maladies—yet now she was glowing, radiant. My first thought on seeing her was that prayers are indeed answered.

As we drove back, Emilio and my wife made small talk in the front while my son and I sat in the back in silence. We dropped them off at a house of some friends of my wife, where she now wanted to live. I went back to the walls that held only their phantoms.

~~~

I sat alone in the cabin, alone except for a mountain of dusty furniture, chairs, mattresses, window frames . . . items that my wife had so excitedly claimed from roadsides and rubbish dumps, items which she imagined would eventually find their meaningful place in the cabin, but instead had left the cabin looking like the dump they came from. The junk was interspersed with random pieces of old underwear, baby clothes and broken toys. In this dusty labyrinth, mice ran around freely during the day, scratched at night and left their droppings everywhere.

Amidst this chaos I sat day after day, night after night. As I sat staring at blank walls, I remembered, that it was here, right where I was sitting, that I first had the vision of that sacred place, the vision of looking out of the natural stone-framed windows, the place that had assured me of peace and healing. The reminder was like a knife twisting in my side. I had broken with my wife and son, travelled half the world over five months, but had not found that place, not found that healing—and now I was right back where I started. I wished I could forget the vision; now it just seemed a symbol of all that had gone wrong.

Occasionally I went to the town to meet acquaintances, to

try and take myself out of my endless questioning, out of my film. But in others, I just watched other films. The change of plot brought the temporary relief of amusement. Yet I felt we were all cowering in our little boxes of reality, boxes that could never feel right, so we would paint them, rotate them, expand them, change them—all so long as we had our box. To fit in there, I too would have to draw my box, because people only felt comfortable interacting with a limited geometry—and that if I didn't draw it, others would define it for me. The box had the comfort of walls, limits to bounce back off, to return us to the familiar. Without a box, what would we be? Empty space perhaps, a space that could permeate everything, everyone—what would there be to differentiate us?

Occasional interactions with acquaintances left an emptiness that gnawed at my guts. I went to cafés and sat alone; I sat alone in the plazas; I stood alone at public events—but it was a terrible loneliness—the loneliness of isolation, of being surrounded by beings in isolation. On returning to my mountain solitude I invariably felt relief. Sitting alone in contemplation, it struck me that during my travels I had visited what many considered the holiest places on the planet. There had been Rishikesh—the home of Yoga, Varanasi—the Hindu's holy city of light, Bhodgaya—the seat of Buddha's enlightenment, and finally I had ended up in Jerusalem! I hadn't planned to go to any of these places! I didn't consider myself a religious person, but somehow fate had taken me from one to the other—and in these great religious centres, I hadn't found religion. Instead, I had found an inexhaustible love for human beings, all-too-human beings with human failings, failings that enabled me, temporarily at least, to forgive my own. If I had passed the time in the presence of perfected beings, maybe I would have only felt more inadequate, felt more dirty—as I had felt after the years of accusations that had been voiced right here, accusations whose echoes still seemed to ring out of the very walls.

I had no appointments, no telephone or media device, and no one came by to visit; completely alone now, I just sat on a mattress on the floor. Uninterrupted, I wandered freely through the crumbling labyrinth of my mind. Sitting day after day amidst the dust of a broken dream, my imagination was given the freedom to be. I became every hero and every villain, every monster and every god, every success and every failure that had ever been suggested of me through the mouths of family, friends and society, of fantasy, of popular media, of dream, and above all, of my wife. With no distractions, I lived all these possibilities of my being and all seemed equally valid. Here, I might go happily insane, I thought, happily insane without bothering anyone.

Day after silent day, I drifted in such contemplation. Mostly, I drifted in and out of my past life—but now it felt as though I were watching it from a distance, like I was watching some other man, like I was watching His Story! I observed His Story as though it were no different from any history which had held my attention. Watching His Story as day turned to night and night turned to day, I realised I could wander through it for eternity if I so chose. Ever changing settings and ever changing characters, friends, enemies, loves, demons, companions, gods and goddesses, all with ever-transforming faces played on the screen of my mind. The same face might take on multiple roles, scenes that never really took place, things I could have done, things I should have done—these scenes all played out equally convincingly. Opportunities not taken advantage of were now heeded and seen through to their conclusions in short time, and yet, the resultant feeling of this altered history left me feeling the same. Even the so-called reruns of reality I wasn't sure of—did I remember it right? Or was I now redirecting his story based on my current feeling? Could I now be viewing history through the eye of another witness, a witness who had been silently present at the event?

As in Rishikesh, as in Bhodgaya, once again the ground seemed to be falling away—the closer I looked at it, the less substance it seemed to have. My identity, it seemed, was defined by divisions . . . my nationality, my profession, my family, my partner, my property . . . my valid reasons for calling trespass, my valid reasons for anger! By explicitly defining what 'I was' I had distanced myself from all that I supposedly 'was not'!

I had always blamed society for the great dis-ease I had felt on playing my limited roles, in forcing me into a scratchy and restrictive suit. But finally, although social authority had coaxed me, it was I that had chosen the suit, only I who had tightened the noose that hung around my collared neck each and every day. From feelings of shame and guilt I had repressed much feeling and imagination, but these had lived on in my sub-conscious and ever beckoned that I wake up to my true self.

Yet seeing it now as I did, no matter how often I dissolved the divisions which that identity implied, they reoccurred—were ever recoursed to as I fled from the Greatest Fear: Being nothing! Becoming nothing!

The foundations I had once tried to build my life upon now appeared only as illusions of the mind, a mind which classified according to form, a mind evolved for individual supremacy, the 'discerning' mind, the mind of Simon! In that mind My *Life* was delimited by an arbitrary border drawn around an assortment of labels, an assortment of choices—a big list of defined fors and againsts—all 'my action' thereby mere automated reaction, eternal re-runs of past evaluations. Within these borders, all events happened in a kind of eternal action-replay—were condemned to occur according to past patterns. Bound by my definitions, I could foresee the rest of a lifetime, could understand that, although scenes and characters would change, that the plot would remain forever the same. In this limited world, the future was as predictable as the past was definable. As this border around *me* now blurred and faded, as my content leaked out, I was left with an ever more frightening challenge—the challenge of utter emptiness.

Weeks went by and I did nothing that I could remember doing and the weeks turned to months. Spring turned to summer and summer to autumn. Seasons passed and I had difficulty separating what had happened from what had happened only in my imagination, which certainly seemed a more eventful place, an ever more real place, more real perhaps than the *external* world.

But still I could not fully accept the emptiness! Once again I felt a mounting urge to run away from it all—to escape! Any shred of an idea had me on my feet . . . Pack my bike and ride off over the Earth! Capitalise on this free time! Dedicate myself to learning an instrument, a language, a new art! Write a book, write poems, write letters to loved ones, get it all down! Go to a nearby town and open my heart to the first soul that welcomes me! Just go to a cave; if you are going to be alone, seeking the depths of your soul, then it should be in a cave! All possible! All endlessly possible!

Over and over, I was on my feet to put whatever was the current great idea in motion, but before I ever made it to the door, I would be assailed by the awareness of all the other possibilities that would thereby be excluded and the questioning would begin again. Ride my bike to where? Via where? Who should I visit en route? What tyres should I use!?

How much time passed like this—plans for great future achievements and journeys to far-flung parts of the planet abandoned after a couple of staggering steps, abandoned before I even left the room in which they were imagined, stopping to stare into the distance, stare into the essence of the Simon who would emerge months or even years later from the consequence of what so nearly just began. This future Simon, with his extra parcel of history, I felt sure, would be in the same place as *me!* There was nowhere left to run I realised, I had already run away from everything, and still, I had never managed to run away from *myself!*

Such imaginary journeys were occasionally punctuated by the vision, once again I saw the rugged stone windows which looked onto the mountains, and for a while, I would once again experience that longed for peace. The more I had the vision, the more I became aware that peace was something I was simply feeling in my own being! I considered that the vision had just been a projection of my mind, what it thought peace should look like! This feeling, I realised, I had also experienced during my travels—had experienced it over and over, experienced it simply as the essence of sharing, sharing with all the shabby angels, all the souls who had bared themselves to me, had enabled me to open my own heart, a heart that I had learned over the preceding years to bury in depths where no light could reach. I became convinced there was no temple to find, nothing to be constructed other than a symbol for what lay beneath.

Rather than far-flung parts of the planet, the excursions I actually made were no further than the wilderness surrounding the cabin. I would suddenly find myself walking near the house, not quite sure how I had gotten there. I would come to where I was when the reruns of history finally ceased, and ceased along with them, the plans for creating a better future.

The mind finally silenced, I felt the enchantment of the ancient chestnut forests, the towering presence of the mountains, the playful ecstasy of the mountain streams. In these there was a vibrancy—an inexplicable sensation of awe—of connection. Looking at the first white flowers of the beanstalk, watching the mist lifting skyward from the silent mountain forest, watching as it spiralled upwards to dissolve in sky, I experienced bliss and knew there was nowhere else to be, nothing more to become.

I had always assumed the Goddess could only take the form of a woman, yet now, as I passed days and weeks on end completely alone in nature, still I sensed Her! Indeed, the longer I spent alone in uninterrupted silence like this, the stronger that presence often became. I realised that She was simply essence, an essence that I sensed from within my own being!

Wandering alone in pristine nature, my mind emptied, I felt Her immanence in the stillness of ancient forests, in the great shafts of sunlight breaking through cloud-strewn skies. I listened to Her song in the babbling of mountain brooks, witnessed Her dance as soft swaying branches in the wind. I felt complete and in love, not in love with any particular thing or person, but simply *in* love.

I felt certain every being had some sense of this, yearned somehow to return to it—this reverence and awe in the presence of natural purity, purity that now exists only in pockets on the planet, that once were overall—all that through long drawn-out efforts, efforts that have been largely unpleasant in themselves, we have enslaved, destroyed and polluted for consumption, for progress. Was I too not part of it all? Was I too not another 'Human Doing'? The last years of my life had proven my efforts to create happiness for myself and others rested on some perverted belief that I might reassemble some of this majesty according to my will, place my manipulating hand on the already divine. Yes, the perfection I now perceived was in pure nature, nature where man had not wielded his tools of destruction.

Still the Voice of Fear had not been fully silenced! 'What

are you going to do?' it cried out! But now I was coming to see all that needed to be done was to fix that which was done before—because now I realised it was always short-sighted—not whole. My creations seemed to lack the perfection I had sought to manifest—a perfection that existed already, the perfection of nature, the perfection of all that has simply been left to be, the perfect beauty of the feminine when her true nature is simply loved.

Once again it was Emilio who blew in as the agent of Karma, of expedience, as the boisterous angel of my destiny. For him, the aftershock of our fateful climb on the stormy face of a wrathful goddess had long worn off. He arrived one Sunday morning raging at the great morass of ignorance and destruction which he knowingly took part in, being a servant of which had brought him none of the promised financial rewards. He seemed to be demanding catharsis—an intensity that would bring the great emotional relief he so badly needed—and one that would simultaneously relieve, at least temporarily, his financial burden. The nature of this catharsis he seemed to imply, lay in my hands. In short—to help him, to help me, there must be something that needed done around the house—today!

I hadn't been planning any work; indeed I hadn't been planning anything; if I was doing anything, it was concentrating on removing my short-sighted will from putting new karma into motion. From months of silence, I felt highly sensitised, like a fine-tuned antenna receiving the subtle energies of all around me, when all around me had been trees, a lonely mountain, the coming and going of squirrels, birds and phantoms of my own creation. Emilio's energy was anything but subtle; he broadcast loud the dire need of destructive effort, to destroy the old and make space for the pure once again to flourish—today!

His energy filled me, hypnotised me; soon, I too was brimming with that destructive need. But what did I need done? I couldn't think of anything that was important. As the need in me grew, pressure quickly built for its exercise. Then I vaguely remembered thinking that it would be nice to have a window upstairs facing the mountains and sunset to the west. I suggested it to Emilio, more as an invitation to a little brainstorming, to play about with it, to feel it out. But none of it! Emilio straight away grabbed a sledgehammer from his van and marched upstairs. A little shakily I went to find my own. When I joined Emilio upstairs, he was drawing hard on a fat joint.

'Donde?' was all he said. 'I don't know. Maybe in the middle?'

'Solo uno?' (Only one?) Emilio asked without any hesitation, as though this were something I must have long drawn up architectural plans for.

'I'm not sure, maybe two.'

'Dos entonces,' he blared impatiently, like he had no tolerance for such indecisiveness.

For the first time, I looked at the wall critically. Three windows would span it.

'Mejor tres, aqui, aqui y aqui.' I indicated an even spacing.

'Vale.'

That was enough. Planning over, Emilio lifted the heavy

sledgehammer and swung it full force against the wall where I had indicated the first window, leaving a crater in the plaster and brickwork, a couple of feet above where I had rested my sleeping head for the last four years. He continued like this as I stood watching transfixed, until he turned to me and pointed to the second window location.

'Tu, alla!' You over there! he ordered indicating the second window position.

Without question, I lifted my sledgehammer and launched it against the same wall. As the head crashed into the white plaster and brickwork behind, I felt a rush of exhilaration. I lifted for another swing, then another, and then I couldn't stop! As both of us flailed heavy sledgehammers with abandon, the room where I had sat immobile for months, where the air itself never moved, that whole room now shook violently like it was experiencing an earthquake. The walls shook, the floorboards shook, maybe we even shook the foundations, but we kept hammering—all concern of consequence was gone; it just felt right!

From inside the dusty tomb of my broken marriage, we hammered. For the pent-up frustrations and disappointments of lifetimes, for the loves that had started laden in beauty and surrender, loves that had promised our salvation but ended in jealously and accusation, we hammered. We hammered until Emilio broke through to the light—at first a tiny finger-size hole—a light that, as it entered, changed the destructive mania that possessed us to something a little finer. Now with a measure of caution and a sense of respect, we worked to frame that light in three large vague rectangles using smaller hammers. All day long we laboured as the light around us grew and grew. We laboured until the light of the setting sun poured into the room.

~~~

I woke up the next morning to find the rubbish heap in which I slept, now covered in an extra layer of debris, the latest cap being broken brick, stone, and concrete shards. The dust lay like a thick carpet among the rubbish dump salvage. The natural light that now filled the room highlighted all the junk and dust that I was spending my days and nights in. Standing there, with this new perspective, for the first time in my life, I felt an overpowering need to clean.

For three weeks I worked without cease. I got up with the first light of dawn and worked through till the last sunset twilight. I started by moving the junk. Into the car it went, then it was returned to the rubbish dump most of it had come from. Then I began to sweep the dust. There was so much of it!—fine dust that had etched its way into every crevice. Each day I would sweep it to my satisfaction, and awake the next morning to see more, the new light highlighting finer and finer layers.

Then I started on the windows. Emilio had helped to blast three gaping holes in the wall, but that had taken only one day and then he had left me without any tools or expertise to patch them up before the fast falling winter.

Without really knowing what I should do, I searched for natural stones in the surrounding forest and cemented them around the holes, often holding them in place until they dried enough to support themselves. Most of the daylight hours, I sat on the terrace roof just beneath the windows, building a mosaic of random stones around their edges. I became deeply absorbed in the work while clouds, rains, mists, and blue skies came and went endlessly. Sunsets often took me by surprise; time itself became elastic. It all reminded me of the sense of meaningful effortlessness I had felt collecting firewood before the birth of my son.

The last thing I did was hang some prayer flags over the top of the windows, and then there was nothing more I could think to do. Weeks had passed; in that time, almost no one had visited and I hadn't gone anywhere else, all the time deeply absorbed in what I was doing. The process had silenced my mind. Now it was finished there was nothing to do but sit down.

So I sat down again where so often I had sat. The weeks of working and cleaning had given my doubting mind a deep rest, had silenced the inner voice that was ever accusing me of inadequacy. As I sat with eyes closed in a transformed space, the forgotten vision of the place of peace that I had first had while sitting on the same spot started to return. At first it returned in brief glimpses—glimpses of the wooden floor, the open space, glimpses of the prayer flags and mountains beyond the stone windows, glimpses that grew and solidified and steadied, until I felt I could almost reach out and touch it all—the clarity grew and grew—until finally my eyes were open.

Letting Go His Story

These are his stories. And if they are his, then what is mine? It's like I am watching the dreams of another—and watching his dreams, I feel love and I feel frustration, I feel whole and I feel empty, I laugh and I cry. Sometimes, I see him proud, jealous, egotistical and weak, and other times, he grows to such proportions that all I perceive seems to be His doing—even I! At these times I merge with him—He and I become one.

I am the wind in the branches. As I blow, the leaves where life force wanes surrender to my promise of transformation. I coax them to let go of the mother that nurtured them to full vibrance. Golden and light as air—on me, they fly and soar and twirl with a freedom they never knew in life. Softly I carry them to the earth and to the river. For some brief moments, flying on spirit in golden dancing ecstasies, they appear as individuals. I carry them to where they will lose form, sometimes gently to the earth, the Great Body from which they sprang; sometimes to the river, where they begin a new journey—a journey which will surely take them to union with all water.

Historians like to stand on the banks of rivers recording for posterity some of the leaves that flow down it. For historians the river that flows is time and the passing leaves are stories. All they can do is record some events that float down. But the whole river cannot be described by some of its content. The river itself runs right now! It runs effortlessly as it has done since time immemorial—and it will probably keep running by the time these vessels we call 'you' and 'I' have disintegrated.

As a tree sheds its leaves, so it lets go all that clung to it and gave it colour, it returns to nakedness. To share our stories is to be no longer concealed by the ephemeral, is to return to innocence. Like the tree, I wish to shed leaves so I might return to nakedness, so that new growth may occur in its season. It is my wish that some leaves may fall into the river, that it will carry my essence once again to yours and yours to mine.

Dedication

What is the soul if not simply the wordless, thoughtless feeling of connection between beings—the sense of deep communion with the other—the knowing of unity, the feeling of overwhelming presence that cannot be ignored, stepped around, or denied. Often, we associate it with a person, a place, a religion . . . or whatever happened to bring it to our awareness in the first place, and then we dedicate to that—and that only—not realising that the face of the soul is in constant transformation. To sew together the torn fragments of the soul, . . . that every piece becomes connected to the whole, that every wave knows it is the ocean, that every one I have loved know that that love lives within me, this is my   dedication.

Acknowledgements

In deciding to publish this book I made the decision to realize a dream and from that moment I found helping hands were all around me. This is not an individual work but a synthesis of the efforts of many. Deep felt gratitude

a Lourdes Nuñez del Rio que en una semana expreso todo el corazon del libro por la magia de su entendimiento y su arte

to Daphna Saker for the cover image, for new visions

to Maria Kilina, богиня, которая всех слушает, for the book cover design

to Megan Crossair for the yoga and for her inspirational comments and for coaxing the silent goddess to the fore

to Aaron Selby for edits, for listening deeply and for helping me realise what I really want

to the inspirations of my life, Santanu, Sushma, Steve, Steffi, Michael and Michael, Paddy, Korbi, Emma, Ana Maria, Kush, Justine, Kamal and Kamal, Katerina, Henry, Jiddu, Freidrich, Gary, Claire, Davy, Tinks, Big Al, Stix, Eammonn, Jesper, Ayelet, Lena, Martin, Gur, Gabi, Ollie, Ralph, Heidi the welsh sunshine, Anna and Jane Meltzer, brother Dan, cousin Mark, Aunt Anne and so many more . . . you are my essence, you are my soul, from you I write

Om Tat Sat!

If you enjoyed this book please I would be most grateful for an honest review on Amazon. Thank you!

By the same Author: **Turning the Wheel : Ireland to India by Bicycle**

At thirty years old, against all sensible advice, I dropped a successful business in website building and pedaled for seven months across Europe, Turkey, Iran, Pakistan, India and Nepal. Eight thousand miles of chaotic highways and empty country lanes, freezing winter-bound mountain passes and steaming tropical jungle paths, vast unpopulated desert highways and the streets of densely packed third world metropolises, brought me from my parents' home in Ireland to the Nepali Himalaya. En route I stayed at the mercy of local inhabitants as I found myself in places well off the tourist radar; with Kurds in goat-hair tea-houses, with respectable Iranians and their opium loaded Shisha pipes, with Afghanis in dirt-floored desert roadhouses and even in the luxurious palace of a desert king and ex-Pakistani president. During these seven months I re-learned to trust the human soul, no matter in what colours it came decked. The great enemy I discovered was internal, the endless solo hours of contemplation bringing fierce challenges my ideas of my own identity. This book is the story of that journ

TURNING THE WHEEL

Simon Loughlin

IRELAND
TO
INDIA
BY
BICYCLE

Printed in Great Britain
by Amazon

48672940R00101